The Spokesman
America's Gulag
Edited by Ken Coates

Published by Spokesman for the Bertrand Russell Peace Foundation

Spokesman 82   2004

CONTENTS

Editorial: America's Gulag	3	*Ken Coates*
Bertrand Russell	8	*James Kirkup*
Dear Mr President...	9	*Irene Khan*
Iraq: Looter's Licence	16	*Ibrahim Warde*
Creative Writing	23	*Kurt Vonnegut*
Vanunu – Free at Last	33	*Bruce Kent*
Peace Dossier	37	*Prisoner abuse in Iraq Tony Blair et al*
		Report of the International Committee of the Red Cross
		Killings of Civilians in Basra and al-'Amara Amnesty International
		More Missing Pages – The Taguba Report
Reviews	95	*Michael Barratt Brown Regan Scott R. Thomas Rae Street*

Printed by the Russell Press Ltd., Nottingham, UK

ISSN 0262 7922   ISBN 0 85124 691 5

Subscriptions
Institutions £30.00/€60/$60
Individuals £20.00 (UK)
                 £25.00 (ex UK)
                 €40/$40

Back issues available on request

A CIP catalogue record for this book is available from the British Library

Published by the
Bertrand Russell Peace Foundation Ltd.,
Russell House
Bulwell Lane
Nottingham NG6 0BT
England
Tel. 0115 9784504
email:
elfeuro@compuserve.com
www.spokesmanbooks.com
www.russfound.org

Editorial Board:
Michael Barratt Brown
Ken Coates
John Daniels
Ken Fleet
Stuart Holland
Tony Simpson

For Peace and Justice, Human Rights and International Solidarity

Bob Crow
General Secretary

Tony Donaghey
President

Editorial

America's Gulag
Full Spectrum Dominance versus Universal Human Rights

'No one shall be subjected to torture or to cruel, inhuman or degrading treatment or punishment.'
Universal Declaration of Human Rights, 1948, Article Five

'How do people get to this clandestine Archipelago? Hour by hour planes fly there, ships steam their course there, and trains thunder off to it…without a mark on them to tell of their destination. And at ticket windows or at travel bureaux…the employees would be astounded if you were to ask for a ticket to go there...Those who go to the Archipelago to administer it get there via the training schools of the Ministry…Those who go there to be guards are conscripted via the military conscription centres.

And those who…go there to die must get there solely and compulsorily via arrest.'
Alexander Solzhenitsyn, *The Gulag Archipelago*, Volume one, chapter one

Twenty miles west of Baghdad lies the Abu Ghraib prison, dank with the memories of Saddam Hussein's most notorious tortures. It was not closed down by the American liberators, but, after having been comprehensively looted immediately after the fall of the regime, stripped of doors, windows, and every moveable object, urgent reconstruction followed. The Americans had the floors tiled, the plumbing refurbished and the walls hosed down. Henceforth it was to be the latest jewel in the crown of the American gulag. Several thousand new prisoners were quickly admitted. They included teenage children and women. By Autumn 2003 they numbered a few thousand, loosely classified in three categories: common criminals; detainees suspected of 'crimes against the coalition'; and a few 'high value' leaders of the uprising against the coalition forces.

Brigadier General Janis Karpinski was designated Commander of the prison, at the same time that she was given responsibility for two other jails. She disposed of a small army: three thousand four hundred army reservists, and eight battalions of regular soldiers. Like her, the reservists had no experience in the administration of prisons. When Major General Antonio M. Taguba came on the scene to investigate 'failures of the army prison system', General Karpinski was obviously nonplussed.

Taguba uncovered a remarkable history of abuse. In the last quarter of 2003, he identified 'sadistic, blatant and wanton criminal' behaviour. Taguba's report has been filtered through into the world press. Detainees had been beaten with broomsticks and chairs, male prisoners had been threatened with rape, or even sodomised with broom handles or chemical lights. Military Alsatian dogs had been unleashed to frighten and maul some detainees. The repulsive photographs of these and other incidents were systematically used to intimidate detainees awaiting interrogation. Subsequently they were to shock the American legislators to whom they were shown.

It was hardly accidental that the management of Abu Ghraib was strengthened by bringing in the Commander of Guantanamo, Major General Geoffrey Miller[1]. And Guantanamo was the inheritor of a large part of the prison population of Bagram in Afghanistan. Today it is alleged that some three hundred people are still detained in Bagram, north of Kabul, and others in Kandahar, Jalalabad and Asadabad. American Special Forces are said to have held other prisoners at Gardez and Khost. Bagram detainees have been continuously shackled, intentionally kept awake for extended periods of time, and forced to assume painful postures for extended periods, according to Human Rights Watch. Some Bagram prisoners were flown to Guantanamo, which imprisons six hundred or more people, brought in from outposts of the American gulag in many different locations. Others were relocated to a CIA interrogation centre in Kabul, according to the *Washington Post*, 'known as "the Pit", named for its despairing conditions'.

Two people were killed during interrogation in Afghanistan, and the Medical Foundation for the Care of Victims of Torture has called for an investigation of the circumstances of their death. Twenty-two-year-old Dilawar and thirty-year-old Mullah Habibullah died during questioning, and their deaths are being treated by the American authorities as 'homicides'. Bagram, of course, is the site where Bob Woodward and other *Washington Post* reporters revealed in December 2002 the practice of 'torture-lite'. We reported at the time their allegations about the regular 'rendering' of prisoners for torture in earnest in the prisons of less fastidious nations, where penal practices were less inhibited by civilised standards.

Dilawar, says the Medical Foundation, 'died on December 10th, the day commemorating the signing of the Universal Declaration of Human Rights, championed by the US since 1948'.

The torture of prisoners, allegedly in pursuit of counter terrorist information, is a direct affront to the Universal Declaration, to the Geneva Conventions, and to all the other international instruments such as the UN Convention Against Torture, and the European Convention, which prohibit torture. But there have been persistent reports of aggravated physical and sexual abuse of prisoners at home in the United States, in Pennsylvania, Arizona and Virginia, where there has never been any pretence of 'seeking information'. Like the Iraqi prisoners, civil prisoners in Virginia have been compelled to wear hoods, while they also suffered beatings and were made to crawl on the ground. But the explanation of such treatment, unlike that in the new Gulag, has nothing to do with patriotism, but much to do with sadism. Nonetheless, techniques appear to be transferable.

Fox Butterfield reported in the *New York Times* that

> 'Some of the worst abuses have occurred in Texas, whose prisoners were under a Federal Consent Decree during much of the time President Bush was Governor, because of crowding and violence by guards against inmates. Judge William Wayne,

Justice of the Federal District Court, imposed the decree after finding that guards were allowing inmate gang leaders to buy and sell other inmates as slaves for sex.

The experts also pointed out that the man who directed the reopening of the Abu Ghraib prison in Iraq last year, and trained the guards there, resigned under pressure as Director of the Utah Department of Corrections in 1997 after an inmate died while shackled to a restraining chair for sixteen hours. The inmate, who suffered from schizophrenia, was kept naked the whole time.

The Utah official, Lane McCotter, later became an executive of a private prison company, one of whose jails was under investigation by the Justice Department when he was sent to Iraq as part of a team of prison officials, prosecutors, and police chiefs, picked by Attorney General John Ashcroft to rebuild the country's criminal justice system.'

If civilian prisoners, the mentally ill, and other victims of the American penal system can be treated in this way, what hope is there for terrorist suspects in the far-flung and inaccessible prisons which have grown up in the America network of bases which girdle the world?

Such bases were numerous during the days of the Cold War. Some, like the immense installations at Okinawa, were unbelievably vast. But far from contracting with the disappearance of the red menace, they have proliferated geographically and grown in scale. Today they are emplaced in one hundred and thirty-two different countries, and have taken over entire islands, which may be closed to all non-military comers. Yesterday there was a noticeable adversary, but now there is none. Within this absence of military rivalry has been secreted the official military doctrine, of 'full spectrum dominance'.

The Department of Defence in the United States stated all this with remarkable economy, in its millennium declaration: *Joint Vision 20/20*:

> 'The ultimate goal of our military force is to accomplish the objectives directed by the National Command Authorities. For the joint force of the future, this goal will be achieved through full spectrum dominance – the ability of US forces operating unilaterally or in combination with multinational and interagency partners, to defeat any adversary and control any situation across the full range of military operations. The full range of operations includes maintaining a posture of strategic deterrence. It includes theatre engagement and presence activities. It includes conflict involving employment of strategic forces and weapons of mass destruction, major theatre wars, regional conflicts, and smaller-scale contingencies. It also includes those ambiguous situations residing between peace and war, such as peacekeeping and peace enforcement operations, as well as non-combat humanitarian relief operations and support to domestic authorities.
>
> The label full spectrum dominance implies that US forces are able to conduct prompt, sustained, and synchronised operations with combinations of forces tailored to specific situations, and with access to and freedom to operate in all domains – space, sea, land, air, and information. Additionally, given the global nature of our interests and obligations, the United States must maintain its overseas presence forces and the ability to rapidly project power world-wide in order to achieve full spectrum dominance.'

Of course, this bold statement can be bent to different purposes, depending on the prevailing political ascendancy. It did not mean the same thing in the more consensual days of some democratic leaders that it does today in the heyday of George Bush's ferocious unilateralism. But at least one western Government outside the United States has been able to follow the transition from the consensual to unilateralism without too much difficulty. Listen to Jack Straw admonishing the House of Commons about the realities of modern military power:

> 'It is the United States which has the military power to act as the world's policeman, and only the United States. We live in a uni-polar world; the United States has a quarter of the world's wealth, the world's GDP, and it has stronger armed forces than the next 27 countries put together. So its predominance is huge. That is a fact. No one can gainsay it; no one can change it in the short or medium term. The choice we have to make in the international community is whether, in a uni-polar world, we want the only super-power to act unilaterally and we force them to act unilaterally or whether we work in such a way that they act within the multilateral institutions. What I say to France and Germany and all the other European Union colleagues is to take care, because just as America helps to define and influence our politics, so what we do in Europe helps to define and influence American politics. We will reap a whirlwind if we push the Americans into a unilateralist position in which they are the centre of this uni-polar world.'

The uncountable bases scattered all around the world certainly contribute to a kind of dominance. But full spectrum brutality does not. Far from it: the revelations about torture in Bagram, Guantanamo and Abu Ghraib, as well as the allegations about rendition to Syria, Egypt, Jordan and Saudi Arabia are arousing a worldwide revulsion which will underpin a very solid movement in defence of human rights.

Ken Coates

Notes

1. 'When Maj. Gen. Geoffrey D. Miller arrived in Iraq last August with a team of military police and intelligence specialists, the group was confronted by chaos. In one prison yard, a detainee was being held in a scorching hot shipping container as punishment, one team member recalled. An important communications antenna stood broken and unrepaired. Prisoners walked around barefoot, with sores on their feet and signs of untreated illness. Garbage was everywhere.

    Perhaps most important, with the insurgency raging in Iraq, there was no effective system at the prisons for wringing intelligence from the prisoners, officials said. "They had no rules for interrogations," a military officer who travelled to Iraq with General Miller said. "People were escaping and getting shot. We tried to offer them some very basic recommendations."

    According to information from a classified interview with the senior military intelligence officer at Abu Ghraib prison, General Miller's recommendations prompted a shift in the interrogation and detention procedures there. Military Intelligence officers were given greater authority in the prison, and military police guards were asked to help gather information about the detainees. Whether those changes contributed to the abuse of prisoners that grew horrifically more serious last fall is now at the centre of the widening prison scandal.

General Miller's recommendations were based in large part on his command of the detention camp in Guantanamo Bay, Cuba, where he won praise from the Pentagon for improving the flow of intelligence from terrorist suspects and prisoners of the Afghanistan war. In Iraq, General Miller's team gave officers at the prisons copies of the procedures that at had been developed at Guantanamo to interrogate and punish the prisoners, according to the officer who travelled with him. Computer specialists and intelligence analysts explained the systems they had used in Cuba to process information and report it back to the United States.'

New York Times, Thursday 13 May 2004

TRANSPORT & GENERAL WORKERS' UNION
South East & East Anglia

Trade Union Rights are Human Rights

- repeal the anti-union laws

Eddie McDermott
Regional Secretary

John Childs
Regional Chair

(phone)
020.8800.4281

(e-mail)
emcdermott@tgwu.org.uk

(fax)
020.8802.8388

BERTRAND RUSSELL

In another February, on a Sunday afternoon eight years ago,
I wept for you, and for a world that could reject your voice.

You were so frail, so ancient; yet stronger than us all.
You stood beside me on a platform in Trafalgar Square
among the toothless lions of a tyrannous imperial pride,
under the shadow of Nelson strutting in the falling snow.

Your head was bare, and your wild white hair
blazed like your mind in the wind of whirling flakes.
Your face, the mask of a tragic hawk,
was sad and bitter as you cried your warnings and defiance
at the armed forces of error, the police of Britain,
the criminal politicians, the priests of power, the insane
manufacturers of arms and poison gas and atom bombs,
inhuman profiteers all, sucking the blood of human misery.

You stood alone before the gathered heads of microphones,
tilted intelligently, raised like vipers, cobras about to strike.
– But like a saint, or like Apollo, god of poetry and music,
you charmed them into peace. You won their love with love,
with the fearless beauty of your mind, your noble voice.

Dear man, I remember your friendship for the lost and helpless,
and the grasp of your withered hand in mine that February day,
delicate but strong. I remember the wise humour of your smile,
twisted yet pure; the sparkle in your hooded, sombre eyes;
the deep lines in your cheeks; the nose like a mountain peak.
– And O, that great and simple brow – so vast, so calm, so full!

Most of all, I remember how you taught me to have courage
to defy the world in solitude; how to disarm
the dangerous stupidity of man, using weapons not of this world –
intellect with love; wit with pity; candour with compassion.

Now, in a foreign snow, my tears are falling for you,
and for the world, that did not heed your warning cries.

James Kirkup
Tokyo, February 3rd 1970

No more Hiroshimas, Poems and Translations by James Kirkup
is newly published by Spokesman Books (price £5).

Dear Mr. President...

On the question of torture and cruel, inhuman or degrading treatment

Irene Khan

The Secretary General of Amnesty International wrote to the President of the United States on 7 May 2004.

Dear Mr President,

The world is watching as your administration responds to the most recent evidence of torture and degrading treatment of Iraqis at the hands of US personnel. While Amnesty International welcomes official statements that the allegations are being taken seriously, the ultimate proof of this will be in actions not words. In this regard, your government's record in the context of 'war on terror' detentions gives cause for concern, as fundamental principles of law and human rights continue to be violated despite the administration's stated commitment to these principles.

Amnesty International recalls your statement on 26 June 2003, made on the occasion of the United Nations International Day in Support of Victims of Torture, in which you said that 'the United States is committed to the worldwide elimination of torture and we are leading this fight by example'. The organization urges you now to ensure that the USA fully meets its international obligations, including as a state party to the Convention against Torture and Other Cruel, Inhuman or Degrading Treatment or Punishment, to investigate all allegations of torture and ill-treatment, publish all findings, prosecute all perpetrators, compensate all victims, and prevent any future torture or cruel, inhuman or degrading treatment. We call on the USA to open the doors of its detention facilities in Iraq, Afghanistan, Guantánamo Bay, and at undisclosed locations elsewhere, to independent bodies, including visits by United Nations Special Rapporteurs.

In July 2003, Amnesty International sent your government a *Memorandum on Concerns Relating to Law and Order* in Iraq. The Memorandum included allegations of torture and ill-treatment of Iraqi detainees by US and Coalition forces.[1] The allegations included beatings, electric shocks, sleep deprivation, hooding, and prolonged forced standing and kneeling. We have never received a response or any indication from the administration or the Coalition Provisional Authority that an investigation took place. Likewise, we have never received a response to the *Memorandum to the US Government on the rights of people in US custody in Afghanistan and Guantánamo Bay* which we sent to you in April 2002, and which also raised concerns about questions and allegations of torture and ill-treatment.[2]

The military investigation in Iraq headed by Major General Antonio Taguba found 'systemic and illegal abuse of detainees' in the Abu Ghraib facility (Baghdad Central Confinement Facility, BCCF) between August 2003 and February 2004, and concluded that soldiers had 'committed egregious acts and grave breaches of international law at Abu Ghraib/BCCF and Camp Bucca, Iraq'. Amnesty International is concerned that the Taguba report was not intended for public release, and that the administration's current response has only come once the report and the photographic evidence came into the public domain.

At the Department of Defense news briefing on 4 May 2004, Secretary of Defense Rumsfeld said that he was 'stunned' by the allegations. In one of several statements apparently downplaying the seriousness of the allegations, however, he added that his 'impression is that what has been charged so far is abuse, which I believe technically is different from torture'. Amnesty International stresses that the 'numerous incidents of sadistic, blatant, and wanton criminal abuse' found by the Taguba investigation constitute acts of torture or cruel, inhuman or degrading treatment, in violation of international law. The Fourth Geneva Convention (Article 147, Convention (IV) relative to the Protection of Civilian Persons in Time of War, Geneva, 12 August 1949) lists 'torture or inhuman treatment', without distinguishing among the two in terms of gravity, among their 'grave breaches'. These are war crimes and are the most serious offences that every High Contracting Party to the Conventions must prevent and suppress, including by prosecuting the perpetrators. The incidents recorded in the Taguba report include:

> Punching, slapping, and kicking detainees; jumping on their naked feet; Videotaping and photographing naked male and female detainees; Forcibly arranging detainees in various sexually explicit positions for photographing; Forcing detainees to remove their clothing and keeping them naked for several days at a time; Forcing naked male detainees to wear women's underwear; Forcing groups of male detainees to masturbate themselves while being photographed and videotaped; Arranging naked male detainees in a pile and then jumping on them; Positioning a naked detainee on a MRE Box, with a sandbag on his head, and attaching wires to his fingers, toes, and penis to simulate electric torture; Writing 'I am a Rapest' (sic) on the leg of a detainee alleged to have forcibly raped a 15-year old fellow detainee, and then photographing him naked; Placing a dog chain or strap around a naked detainee's neck and having a female Soldier pose for a picture; A male MP guard having sex with a female detainee; Using military working dogs (without muzzles) to intimidate and frighten detainees, and in at least one case biting and severely injuring a detainee.

Major General Taguba also found 'credible' evidence that the following abuses took place:

Breaking chemical lights and pouring the phosphoric liquid on detainees; Threatening detainees with a charged 9mm pistol; Pouring cold water on naked detainees; Beating detainees with a broom handle and a chair; Threatening male detainees with rape; Allowing a military police guard to stitch the wound of a detainee who was injured after being slammed against the wall in his cell; Sodomizing a detainee with a chemical light and perhaps a broom stick.

The Taguba report emphasized that the findings were 'amply' supported by confessions from suspected perpetrators, statements from detainees and witnesses, as well as 'extremely graphic photographic evidence'.

The report found that there was a failure to establish clear training, procedures and oversight on interrogation and treatment of detainees, and 'that very little instruction or training' was provided to military police personnel on the applicable rules of the Geneva Conventions.

At the 4 May Pentagon briefing to respond to the allegations, Secretary Rumsfeld maintained that 'the fact is, this is an exception', and added that 'there may be things that we can do that would be helpful in helping the world understand that this is an exceptional situation; it is not a pattern or a practice.' Although he acknowledged that there 'are allegations of abuse in various other locations', he added that 'at any given time there are always allegations and charges of abuse in detention facilities' and that there 'is a pattern and a practice of terrorists to allege abuse'.

A pattern of abuse

During the past two years, consistent allegations of brutality and cruelty by US agents against detainees, including in Iraq and Afghanistan, have been presented by Amnesty International and others at the highest levels of the US Government, including the White House, the Department of Defense, and the Department of State.

Numerous people who have been held in the US Air Bases in Bagram and Kandahar in Afghanistan have spoken of the torture or other cruel, inhuman or degrading treatment to which they say they were subjected in US custody in Afghanistan.[3] For example, former Guantánamo detainee Wazir Mohammad recalled to Amnesty International in February 2004 his detention in US custody in Afghanistan in 2002. He spoke of the excessive and cruel use of shackles and handcuffs, sleep deprivation, and of being forced to crawl on his knees from his cell to the interrogation room, a crawl of about 10 minutes. His testimony echoes that of numerous other former detainees.

As with hundreds if not thousands of other detainees, during his whole time in Bagram and Kandahar, Wazir Mohammad was held incommunicado. He was given no opportunity to challenge the lawfulness of his detention. He had no lawyer, no access to his family, and was not brought before any court, including the 'competent tribunal' envisaged by the Geneva Conventions to determine prisoner status in time of war. He never met a delegate from the International Committee of the Red Cross (ICRC) either. During more than a year in Guantánamo he says he met an ICRC delegate once, on the first day.

Last month in Yemen, Amnesty International spoke with another former

Guantánamo prisoner, Walid al-Qadasi. He recalled his time in a secret detention facility in Kabul, interrogated by US agents. He said that the first night of interrogation had been coined by the prisoners as 'the black night'. He told Amnesty International that: 'They cut our clothes with scissors, left us naked and took photos of us, before they gave us Afghan clothes to wear. They then handcuffed our hands behind our backs, blindfolded us and started interrogating us...They threatened me with death, accusing me of belonging to *al-Qa'ida*. They put us in an underground cell measuring approximately two metres by three metres. There were ten of us in the cell. We spent three months in the cell... During the three month period in the cell, we were not allowed outside into the open air.' He alleged that the detainees were subjected to sleep deprivation, including by the use of loud music.

Incommunicado detention facilitates torture and ill-treatment. In his report to the UN Commission on Human Rights in 2004, the Special Rapporteur on torture 'reiterates the recommendation of his two predecessors and urges all States to declare incommunicado detention illegal'. The Special Rapporteur added that 'incommunicado detention is aggravated when individuals are held in secret places of detention' and that 'it should be a punishable offence for any official to hold a person in a secret and/or unofficial place of detention'.

The USA cannot claim to be leading the struggle against torture by example, when the example it is setting is one of using prolonged incommunicado detention, including in undisclosed locations. Transparency, access and accountability are the most effective measures against torture and ill-treatment. The USA should employ these measures and truly lead by example.

Amnesty International has previously expressed concern about the mixed messages which the US government has sent regarding its commitment to international human rights standards. In June 2003, the administration issued a strong statement that government policy was to 'comply with all of its legal obligations in its treatment of detainees, and in particular with legal obligations prohibiting torture'.[4] At the same time it has failed to comply with the Geneva Conventions with regard to the Guantánamo detainees.[5] When the USA unilaterally decides whether or not to affirm the rights of individuals protected by international treaties and agreements, this may send a message to troops and others that the government is set on a course in which international agreements can be ignored or set aside at the discretion of the executive for the sake of expediency.

Intelligence and interrogation

Amnesty International has also recently spoken to a person who has worked in Guantánamo who has said that most if not all the detainees he had contact with there (approximately 40) had alleged that they were physically abused in Kandahar or Bagram. Based on this knowledge, this person expressed no surprise at the recent evidence emerging from Iraq, and stated that the abuse in Afghanistan appeared to be part of softening up detainees for interrogation and detention.

The Taguba report presents evidence that the abuse allegedly inflicted on the detainees in Iraq followed requests from military intelligence and other government interrogators that the military police (MP) guards in the prison 'set physical and mental conditions for favourable interrogation of witnesses'. Guards alleged that military intelligence personnel had given instructions including 'loosen this guy up for us', 'make sure he has a bad night'; 'make sure he gets the treatment'; and 'Good job, they're breaking down real fast. They answer every question. They're giving out good information, Finally, and Keep up the good work. Stuff like that.'

At a Coalition Provisional Authority Briefing in Iraq on 4 May 2004, Major General Geoffrey Miller stated that while physical contact between interrogator and detainees is prohibited, 'sleep deprivation and stress positions and all that could be used. But they must be authorized'. The United Nations Committee against Torture, the expert body established by the Convention against Torture and Other Cruel, Inhuman or Degrading Treatment or Punishment has expressly held that restraining detainees in very painful positions, hooding, threats, and prolonged sleep deprivation are methods of interrogation which violate the prohibition on torture and cruel, inhuman or degrading treatment.

Amnesty International notes that Major General Miller commanded the Guantánamo detention operation until he was recently put in charge of detainee operations in Iraq. The Taguba report notes that from '31 August to 9 September 2003, MG Miller led a team of personnel experienced in strategic interrogation to [Iraq] to review current Iraq Theater ability to rapidly exploit internees for actionable intelligence'. The Taguba report also noted that Major General Miller's team had stated that 'it is essential that the guard force be actively engaged in setting the conditions for successful exploitation of the internees.' It seems that the alleged torture and ill-treatment at the centre of the Taguba report began around this time.

The Taguba report holds that 'Military Police should not be involved with setting "favourable conditions" for subsequent interviews. These actions…clearly run counter to the smooth operation of a detention facility.'

Access for human rights monitors

The US administration has denied access to independent human rights monitors, including Amnesty International, to places of detention. We again recall your statement of 26 June 2003, promising the USA's commitment to eradicating torture, in which you said: 'Notorious human rights abusers, including, among others, Burma, Cuba, North Korea, Iran, and Zimbabwe, have long sought to shield their abuses from the eyes of the world by staging elaborate deceptions and denying access to international human rights monitors.' We urge you to ensure such access is granted now, to all US detention facilities.

While the International Committee of the Red Cross has had access to detainees, even this access is reported not to have been full and ongoing in some instances, including in Bagram Air Base, and at undisclosed locations elsewhere. In this regard, we are concerned by the following entry in the Taguba report:

> The various detention facilities operated by the 800th MP Brigade have routinely held persons brought to them by Other Government Agencies (OGAs) without accounting for

them, knowing their identities, or even the reason for their detention. The Joint Interrogation and Debriefing Center (JIDC) at Abu Ghraib called these detainees 'ghost detainees.' On at least one occasion, the 320th MP Battalion at Abu Ghraib held a handful of 'ghost detainees' (6-8) for OGAs that they moved around within the facility to hide them from a visiting International Committee of the Red Cross (ICRC) survey team. This maneuver was deceptive, contrary to Army Doctrine, and in violation of international law.

Deaths in custody

Two men who died in US custody in December 2002 in Bagram Air Base in Afghanistan had not been seen by the International Committee of the Red Cross. The official autopsies recorded the cause of their deaths as 'homicide' and found 'blunt force injuries' in both cases. Amnesty International was informed by Chief of Public Affairs at the US Army Criminal Investigation Command on 6 May 2004 that the investigations into their deaths are continuing but that the investigation 'is close to completion'. It is now 17 months since the two men died. Investigations into another dozen cases of deaths in US custody in Iraq and Afghanistan are reported to be underway.

Amnesty International repeats here one of the allegations made in the journal of Staff Sergeant Ivan L. Frederick concerning a death in custody of an Iraqi prisoner in Abu Ghraib: 'They stressed him out so bad that the man passed away. They put his body in a body bag and packed him in ice for approximately 24 hours in the shower… The next day the medics came in and put his body on a stretcher, placed a fake IV in his arm and took him away.' Frederick stated that the prisoner had never been recorded in the prison system 'and therefore never had a number'.

We emphasise that all deaths in custody must be investigated and that the results of all these investigations must be made public. If anyone is found to have died as a result of torture, his or her dependants would be entitled to compensation, under Article 14 of the Convention against Torture. Those found responsible must be brought to justice.

Amnesty International's recommendations

Amnesty International urges the US Government to:
– investigate the allegations at Abu Ghraib prison, Iraq, and other detention facilities to establish whether war crimes have been committed and ensure accountability at the highest level;
– bring to justice those responsible for war crimes and other violations in accordance with the USA's obligations under international and US law. Such investigations should not just cover the direct perpetrators, but must include the higher chain of command responsibility;
– initiate investigations into all other allegations of abuse of detainees held in US custody in Iraq, Afghanistan and elsewhere;
– suspend from duties any public officials involved pending the outcome of the investigation and any subsequent legal or disciplinary proceedings;
– ensure, through appropriate policies, training and oversight, that torture or

other cruel, inhuman or degrading treatment will not be tolerated. All detainees in US custody must be treated humanely and in accordance with US obligations under international human rights and humanitarian law;
- launch a full investigation into interrogation practices of detainees in US custody wherever they are held around the world and make the findings public;
- prohibit all techniques during interrogations which violate the prohibition against torture or other cruel, inhuman or degrading treatment. These include such techniques as holding detainees naked, making them assume painful positions, sleep deprivation, exposure to extreme cold, and hooding;
- ensure that private contractors uphold US and international law, and that they receive adequate training on human rights practices and protections.
- end the practice of incommunicado detention. Provide immediate access to detainees to their families and lawyers, ensure regular access to the ICRC in all places of detention and access for independent human rights organizations, including representatives of Amnesty International, into detention facilities;
- invite the United Nations experts covering torture and arbitrary detention to immediately visit US detention facilities in Iraq and wherever else they may seek such a visit.
- make use of the services of the International Humanitarian Fact-Finding Commission provided for by Article 90 of Additional Protocol I of the Geneva Conventions to look into the allegations of abuse and related US investigations.
- ensure that any victims of torture or inhumane treatment receive full reparations, including compensation, as required under international law.

I trust that you will give due consideration to the concerns raised in this letter.
Yours sincerely
Irene Khan
Secretary General
cc Secretary of Defense Donald Rumsfeld
Secretary of State Colin Powell

Notes
1 http://web.amnesty.org/library/Index/ENGMDE141572003
2 http://web.amnesty.org/library/Index/ENGAMR510532002
3 See USA: The threat of a bad example: Undermining international standards as 'war on terror' detentions continue, AI Index: AMR 51/114/2003, August 2003, http://web.amnesty.org/library/Index/ENGAMR511142003 USA: Undermining security: Violations of human dignity, the rule of law and the National Security Strategy in 'war on terror' detentions, AI Index: AMR 51/061/2004, 9 April 2004
http://web.amnesty.org/library/Index/ENGAMR510612004
4 Letter to US Senator Patrick J Leahy from William J. Haynes, dated 25 June 2003
5 Amnesty International and others, including the ICRC, have repeatedly expressed concern that none of the detainees has been brought before a 'competent tribunal' to determine his status, as required by Article 5 of the Third Geneva Convention.

Copyright©Amnesty International

Iraq: Looter's Licence

Ibrahim Warde

Ibrahim Warde is research affiliate at the Centre for International Studies, Massachusetts Institute of Technology (Cambridge, Massachusetts) and author of The Financial War on Terror *(forthcoming from I B Tauris, London).*

The Economist described the legal and institutional groundwork laid down by Iraq's Coalition Provisional Authority (CPA) as 'a capitalist dream ... The kind of wish-list that foreign investors and donor agencies dream of for developing markets.' This dream was fulfilled with decrees signed by United States proconsul Paul Bremer[1]. Income and corporate taxes were capped at 15%; tariffs were eliminated (though 5% reconstruction surcharge was imposed on certain imports); the monetary and financial system was overhauled; and some 200 public companies were to be privatised. After more than 40 years of strict government control Iraq was, at least on paper, transformed into a vast free trade zone.

The shock therapy was justified in either-or terms by the US Defence Secretary, Donald Rumsfeld, whose agency oversees the reconstruction effort: 'Market systems will be favoured, not Stalinist command systems'[2]. The most controversial reform was the regulation, or rather non-regulation, of foreign investment: on 19 September Order 39 threw open once heavily guarded doors to foreign investment: foreigners could now own property and invest in any sector of the Iraqi economy with the exception of natural resources. The decree made no provisions for prior authorisation or screening mechanisms. Foreign investors would need no local partners; there was no obligation of local reinvestment. The foreign investment regime became more liberal than those of the United States or Britain, where certain sectors including armaments and media are off-limits to foreigners. It went beyond World Bank guidelines on the treatment of foreign direct investment, which recognise the right to maintain mechanisms governing admission of foreign investment and allow for reasonable limits on repatriation of revenues.

The reform, hailed by the Coalition Provisional Authority as 'setting the most far-sighted investment climate in the Middle East', did everything to please the investment community, although some still considered it insufficiently bold. Harvard economist Robert Barro, while acknowledging the 'nobility' of reforms anchored in 'law and private property', deplored the way the oil industry was considered as 'owned in common' and kept off-limits to foreign investors[3]. A major law firm lamented the fact that 'record-keeping and maintenance of accounting records [had to be] in Arabic'[4].

Despite such reservations, the international business community was euphoric. Colossal contracts were about to be handed out. Iraq, as the world's second largest oil producer, offered limitless possibilities. There was talk of deals of the century, a gold rush, a free enterprise heaven. The country was to become the first Islamic tiger – a model and showcase for the entire Middle East.

Many people wonder whether this reform would survive a return to full Iraqi sovereignty. The legality of such reforms is in question. According to the Hague Regulations of 1907 and to the Fourth Geneva Convention of 1949, an occupying power has no right to conduct sweeping reforms. It should be said that such considerations do not seem to preoccupy President George Bush, who, when asked about the compatibility of certain US decisions with international law, responded: 'International law? I better call my lawyer'[5].

The issue was taken seriously by legal experts. A memo written in March 2003 by the British attorney general, Lord Goldsmith, to the prime minister, Tony Blair – and later leaked to the *New Statesman* – warned that 'the imposition of major structural economic reforms' might violate international law unless the Security Council of the United Nations specifically authorised it[6]. Lord Goldsmith, the government's chief legal adviser, was referring to Article 43 of the Hague Regulations, which stipulates that an occupying power must 're-establish and ensure, as far as possible, public order and safety, while respecting, unless absolutely prevented, the laws in force in the country'[7].

Since the fall of Saddam Hussein the Coalition Provisional Authority seems to have done the opposite. Rather than re-establishing public order and safety (judging by the widespread looting and serious unrest), it put considerable effort into overhauling the system. Of course, the question of Iraq's economic future, poorly conceived and badly executed, had been debated for a long time. According to the former treasury secretary Paul O'Neill, from the first days of the Bush administration, long before the 11 September 2001 attacks, there was planning for the best way to control Iraq's lucrative oil contracts[8].

Key members of that administration (including the President, Vice-President Richard Cheney and National Security Adviser Condoleeza Rice) had some experience in the oil industry. Iraq, a potentially rich country devastated by the combined effects of a dreadful dictatorship, three wars and 12 years of international sanctions, was an inviting target. Of course, it was assumed that Iraq would welcome its liberators with flowers.

Post-war pacification has proved far more difficult than anticipated and there are now signs that policy change is likely. In autumn 2003, after two years of 'spiteful unilateralism', the US seemed eager to mend fences with the international community; on 16 October 2003 UN Resolution 1511 legitimising the US presence in Iraq was approved unanimously; on 23 October a donors' conference met in Madrid under the aegis of the United Nations, with 73 countries, 20 international organisations and 13 non-governmental organisations represented.

This conference, described by US officials as a tremendous success, ended with promised commitments of $33bn – in reality, a rough estimate of loans and donations, linked aid (contingent on awarding contracts to national companies), and conditional contributions (which would materialise only with a return to normality or to Iraqi sovereignty). It was far less than the $56bn over four years deemed necessary by the World Bank to get the country back on its feet. Still, the United States could finally boast of the support of the international community.

A few days later, to finance wars in Iraq and Afghanistan, the US Congress approved an $87bn budget, of which $18.6bn would be related to Iraqi military and reconstruction contracts. An amendment providing for criminal penalties against war profiteers was rejected in conference. One of its sponsors, Democratic Senator Richard Durbin, said: 'That's a sad commentary, because I think the American people, as troubled as they are by this $87bn shock, are troubled even more at the prospect that this is going to go to the friends of the administration or to some chummy arrangement or, frankly, be wasted in the deserts of Iraq when it might have been spent for the good of the people of that country.'

On 5 December 2003 Bush announced that James Baker, who had been secretary of state during his father's presidency, would visit European capitals, including Paris, Berlin and Moscow, to negotiate the reduction of the Iraqi debt, which was valued at $130bn. As it had been contracted by a tyrant, it could be considered an 'odious debt' and an unfair burden on the Iraqi people. Such debt reduction was seen as necessary for the reconstruction effort. The selection of Baker, a committed multilateralist, was perceived as another sign that the neo-conservatives were losing ground in Washington.

But the hawks' response was swift. On the same day the defence undersecretary, Paul Wolfowitz, issued a circular announcing that certain countries, among them France, Germany, Russia and Canada, would not be eligible for the main reconstruction contracts, valued at $18.6bn; 26 contracts for the reconstruction effort, to train and equip the new Iraqi army and rebuild the infrastructure, including roads, oil fields, sewers, water and power plants, would be reserved for the 63 countries of the coalition of the willing that had supported the war effort.

Wolfowitz, theoretician of the neo-conservative movement and principal architect of the Iraqi adventure, had again seized the offensive, placing a *fait accompli* before administration moderates. A year earlier the Secretary of State, Colin Powell, had warned opponents to the war that they would face unspecified consequences. It was payback time.

In the circular, Wolfowitz claimed that such measures were 'indispensable for national security and national defence purposes' and that they were intended both as reward and incentive for future cooperation. There was a predictable outcry in the excluded countries, as well as in Washington. The European Union asserted that such measures violated World Trade Organisation rules on public contracts, which ban discrimination against foreign companies on the basis of nationality. Senator Joseph Biden of Delaware, the top Democrat on the Senate Foreign Relations committee, issued a statement criticising the Pentagon move as a 'totally gratuitous slap ... that does nothing to protect our security interests and everything to alienate countries we need with us in Iraq'.

The White House seemed to side with the hawks; its spokesman, Scott McClellan, said: 'I think it is appropriate and reasonable that prime contracts for reconstruction funded by US taxpayer dollars should go to the Iraqi people and those countries who are working with the US on the difficult task of helping to build a free, democratic and prosperous Iraq.'

The State Department argued that the new policy did not intend to exclude, but to include, since besides the United States, 62 countries were eligible for contracts, among them the UK, Italy, Spain and Poland, Rwanda, Palau and Tonga. And the Pentagon added that the list of coalition partners was still open: whoever wished to join was welcome[9]. A spokesman for the US trade representative, Robert Zoellick, rejected accusations of protectionism. Displaying a selective approach to international law, he said the Coalition Provisional Authority was not covered by the World Trade Organisation rules, and that it was free to discriminate in the awarding of contracts as it saw fit.

The most candid policy statement came from President Bush, who declared: 'What I'm saying is, in the expenditure of the taxpayers' money ... the US people, the taxpayers, understand why it makes sense for countries that risked lives to participate in the contracts in Iraq. It's very simple. Our people risked their lives, friendly coalition folks risked their lives and therefore the contracting is going to reflect that.' Until then, the administration had been quiet about mercantile aspects of the Iraqi war, expounding instead on the imminent threat of weapons of mass destruction, or the need to bring democracy to the Iraqi people[10]. Then the president acknowledged what had long been obvious: big contracts were spoils of war and dividends had to be commensurate with the war effort.

That makes it easier to understand the dark side of reconstruction. Every day there is a report of conflicts of interest, fraud, over-billing, botched work, waste or abuse. At the top of the list of profiteers are a few US firms with close ties to the Bush administration. The dominance of US firms in the rebuilding of Iraq has troubled even the most loyal allies. Despite all their efforts, British companies have missed out completely on oil rehabilitation contracts. Trying to head off domestic political embarrassment, the British government has been working behind the scenes, apparently to no avail, to land at least a few face-saving affirmative action contracts[11].

According to a report issued by the Centre for Public Integrity, the 71 companies that received contracts for work in either Iraq or Afghanistan contributed more than $500,000 to Bush's 2000 election campaign. He received more contributions from these sources than any other politician in the past 12 years. According to the report, 'Nearly 60% of the companies had employees or board members who either served in or had close ties to the executive branch for Republican and Democratic administrations, for members of Congress of both parties, or at the highest levels of the military.' In the words of Charles Lewis, the centre's director: 'No single agency supervised the contracting process for the government. This situation alone shows how susceptible the contracting system is to waste, fraud and cronyism'[12].

Despite promises of transparency, the most lucrative contracts were not subjected to public bidding. The main beneficiaries were Halliburton, the oil services company, primarily through its subsidiary Kellogg, Brown and Root (KBR), and construction giant Bechtel, both companies closely tied to the Washington hawks and both with some recent Iraqi experience. Bechtel had built a major pipeline in Iraq, which had been negotiated by Donald Rumsfeld (then special envoy to Iraq) and Saddam Hussein in 1983 when former executives of Bechtel held key positions in the Reagan cabinet. As for Halliburton, whose president from 1995-2000 was the current US vice-president, Richard Cheney, it had been able to operate in Iraq until recently despite a strict international sanctions regime.

An incessant stream of revelations has made Halliburton a symbol of US-style crony capitalism. Henry Waxman, a Democratic member of the House of Representatives from California, has been investigating the cosy ties between Halliburton and US policy-makers. He revealed that a no-bid contract awarded by the US Army Corps of Engineers to its Kellogg, Brown and Root subsidiary in the early days of the war, ostensibly to fight oil fires, was far more extensive. It included an open-ended arrangement to operate oil facilities and distribute oil products, in effect granting the company a concession on substantial Iraqi oil reserves.

According to Waxman, the contract was financed with funds drawn from the oil-for-food programme (renamed the Development Fund for Iraq). Many laws and regulations seem to have been written specifically to protect major oil companies; on 22 May 2003 Bush signed Executive Order 13303, which appears to give them blanket immunity. The decree stated that 'the threat of attachment or judicial process against the Development Fund for Iraq, Iraqi petroleum and petroleum products, and interests therein constitutes an unusual and extraordinary threat to the national security and foreign policy of the United States'. According to Tom Devine, legal director of the Government Accountability Project, 'translated from the legalese, this is a licence for corporations to loot Iraq and its citizens'. He added that the decree 'cancels the concept of corporate accountability and abandons the rule of domestic and international law'[13].

Besides legal risk, Halliburton and its subsidiary were protected against financial risk; their contracts were negotiated on a cost-plus or 'indefinite quantity/indefinite delivery' basis. Under this method, which is justified by conditions of urgency or uncertainty, the company passes all its costs on to the government plus a profit margin typically between 1-7%[14].

Clearly such a system opens the door to abuses and conflicts of interest.

Kellogg, Brown and Root was repeatedly caught red-handed. It was discovered that Kellogg, Brown and Root had inflated the price of petrol imported into Iraq by more than 60%: a gallon bought for 70 cents in Kuwait was sold to the US army for $1.59. The loss to the government was around $61m. Kellogg, Brown and Root's explanation was that the price was justified by transportation costs (although Kuwait is Iraq's neighbour) and high risks. A few weeks later, Kellogg, Brown and Root was caught over-billing the army for $16m for meals for US soldiers. In an unrelated inquiry, a Pentagon audit revealed that the quality of the work of Kellogg, Brown and Root, and of Bechtel, was shoddy[15]. This may be just the tip of the iceberg.

The Pentagon's response to these and other scandals was to open inquiries, create new auditing structures, promise more transparency, and withhold for the time being payment of disputed bills. But the central role of Kellogg, Brown and Root in Iraq was never in question: just as the public learned about dubious practices, Kellogg, Brown and Root received more contracts, generating revenues at the expense of the Iraqi people and the US taxpayer. One of the beneficiaries will be Cheney, who still receives deferred income from Halliburton ($150,000 in 2001, $160,000 in 2002 and $178,000 in 2003) and holds 433,000 stock options whose value is directly influenced by revenues generated by such contracts[16].

The line between politics and business is getting blurred. Iraqi contracts were, at least until the most recent insurrections, considered certain to lead to instant riches. Richard Perle took full advantage of his double role: as the head of the US Defence Policy Board, he was one of the most effective advocates of the extension of the war on terror to Iraq and other countries. As a private citizen, he enriched himself by founding Trireme International, a venture capital firm designed to benefit from his inside knowledge of defence[17]. Joe Allbaugh, Bush's campaign chairman in 2000, created New Bridge Strategies to help corporations obtain contracts in Iraq. The law firm that Douglas Feith (Pentagon undersecretary and leading hawk in charge of supervising the Iraqi reconstruction effort) once worked for has opened in Baghdad.

Comparable conflicts of interest will be common in Iraq. At the end of 2003 the Coalition Provisional Authority had announced that out of 115 identified projects, 25 would be awarded to Iraqi firms. But given the conditions created by Order 39, it will be far from a level playing field. It is anticipated that contracts will be grabbed by insiders and by people close to the Coalition Provisional Authority, or to the Iraqi Governing Council, whose 25 members were named by the Americans.

So what about the Iraqi people? In the official rhetoric, they will be the ultimate beneficiaries of the new order. US officials have been encouraging them to take advantage of the new climate of economic freedom. During a brief trip to Iraq, the Commerce Secretary, Don Evans, said he saw phenomenal progress in the country and praised the entrepreneurial spirit he witnessed. To star CNN journalist Wolf Blitzer he said: 'I stopped by the side of the road to buy some Coca-Cola from some boy, a young entrepreneur'[18].

For the average Iraqi, there is no cause yet for celebration. The injection of substantial funds in a sick economy has exacerbated post-war economic problems. Inflation, rationing, oil shortages and rising unemployment have fed chaos and insecurity. Job cuts in public firms and the disbanding of the Iraqi military have swelled the ranks of the unemployed. The ultra-liberal economic reforms, which allow for labour to be freely imported and profits to be freely repatriated, have had some perverse effects.

Public officials have repeatedly affirmed that unrest is caused by infiltrated foreign elements, but relations between international firms and Iraqis were marked by mistrust from the start. The best illustration is Kellogg, Brown and Root; this over-billing subsidiary of Halliburton relies on Saudi subcontractors to cater for the troops, and much of their workforce is imported from India and Bangladesh. Why do they not employ Iraqis? Because they fear Iraqis may try to poison the troops[19].

Notes

1 *The Economist*, 25 September 2003.
2 Daphne Eviatar, *The New York Times*, 10 January 2004.
3 Robert J Barro, *Business Week*, 5 April , 2004.
4 Pillsbury Winthrop LLP, *International Trade News Brief*, 'Reconstruction of Iraq', 23 September, 2003.
5 *Washington Post*, 12 December 2003.
6 John Kampfner, *New Statesman*, 26 May 2003.
7 Alan Audi, 'Iraq's New Investment Law and the Standard of Civilisation', *Georgetown Law Journal*, vol 93, issue 1, Washington 2004.
8 Ron Suskind, *The Price of Loyalty: George W Bush, the White House, and the Education of Paul O'Neill*, Simon and Schuster, New York, 2004.
9 *Washington Post*, 10 December 2003.
10 Ibrahim Warde, 'It's the economy, stupid', *Le Monde diplomatique*, English language edition, April 2003.
11 Terry Macalister, *The Guardian*, 13 February 2004.
12 http://www.publicintegrity.org/wow/...
13 http://www.whistleblower.org
14 George Anders and Susan Warren, *The Wall Street Journal*, 19 January 2004.
15 Paul Krugman, *New York Times* , 16 December 2003.
16 Halliburton stock peaked at $54.69 in September 2000 and hit a low of $9.10 in July 2002. It now hovers around $30.
17 Revelations about his activities led him first to resign as chairman of the board, and later to leave the board altogether.
18 *Wolf Blitzer Reports*, CNN, 19 October 2003.
19 *The Economist*, 9 October 2003.

With grateful acknowledgements to *Le Monde diplomatique's* English language edition (website: www.mondediplo.com).

All rights reserved © 1997-2004 Le Monde diplomatique

Creative Writing

Kurt Vonnegut

Thank you.

I am happy to be here in Spokane again. I made a fool of myself onstage at Gonzago many years ago now. I was so innocent back then that I still considered it possible that we could become the humane and reasonable America so many members of my generation used to dream of. We dreamed of such an America during the Great Depression, when there were no jobs. And then we fought and often died for that dream during the Second World War, when there was no peace.

But I know now that there is not a chance in hell of America's becoming humane and reasonable. That is because power corrupts us, and absolute power corrupts us absolutely. Human beings are chimpanzees who get crazy drunk on power. I myself have experienced that intoxication. I was once a Corporal.

By saying our leaders are power-drunk chimpanzees, am I in danger of wrecking the morale of our men and women fighting and dying in the Middle East? Their morale, like so many of their bodies, is already shot to pieces. They are being treated, as I never was, like toys a rich kid got for Christmas.

But I will say this:

No matter how corrupt and greedy our government and our corporations and our media and Wall Street and our religious and charitable organizations may become, the music will still be perfectly wonderful.

If I should die, God forbid, let this be my epitaph:

THE ONLY PROOF HE NEEDED
OF THE EXISTENCE OF GOD
WAS MUSIC.

And I have arranged for a Strauss waltz to be played as you depart, so you can waltz the heck out of here when it's time to go. For those of you who don't know how to waltz, nothing could be easier and more human. You go step,

Kurt Vonnegut instructed students at Eastern Washington University, Spokane on 17 April 2004.

slide, rest, step, slide, rest, step, slide, rest. Oom, pah, pah, oom, pah, pah.

Bill Gates doesn't seem to realize that we are dancing animals.

During our catastrophically idiotic war in Vietnam, the music just kept getting better and better. We lost that war, by the way. Order couldn't be restored in Indo-China until the locals finally kicked us the hell out of there.

And how come the people in countries we invade can't fight like ladies and gentlemen, in uniforms, and with tanks and helicopter gunships?

About music: I like Strauss and Mozart and all that, but I would be remiss not to mention the absolutely priceless gift which African-Americans gave to the whole wide world when they were still in slavery…I mean 'the blues'. All pop music today, jazz, swing, be-bop, Elvis Presley, the Beatles, the Stones, rock-and-roll, hip-hop and on and on is derived from the blues.

A gift to the world? One of the best rhythm-and-blues combos I ever heard was three guys and a girl from Finland, playing in a club in Krakow, Poland.

The wonderful writer Albert Murray, who is a jazz historian among other things, told me that, during the era of slavery in this country, an atrocity from which we can never fully recover, the suicide rate per capita among slave owners was much higher than the suicide rate among slaves. Al Murray says he thinks this was because slaves had a way of dealing with depression, which their white owners did not. They could play the blues. He says something else which also sounds right to me. He says the blues can't drive depression clear out of a house, but they can drive it into corners of any room where they are being played.

I am, incidentally, Honorary President of the American Humanist Association, having succeeded the late, great science fiction writer Isaac Asimov in that utterly functionless capacity. We humanists behave as honourably as we can without any expectation of rewards or punishment in an afterlife. We serve as best we can the only abstraction with which we have any real familiarity, which is our community.

We had a memorial service for Asimov a while back, and at one point I said, 'Isaac is up in Heaven now'. That was the funniest thing I could have said to an audience of Humanists. I rolled them in the aisles. It was several minutes before order could be restored.

If I should ever die, again God forbid, I hope some of you will say, 'Kurt's up in Heaven now.' That's my favorite joke.

How do Humanists feel about Jesus? If what he said was superb, how can it matter whether he was God or not?

When you get to my age, if you get to my age, which is eighty-one, and if you have reproduced, you will find yourself asking your own children, who are themselves middle-aged, what life is all about. I have seven kids, four of them adopted. Most of you here are the same age as my grandchildren. They, like you, are being royally shafted and lied to by our Baby Boomer corporations and government.

I put my big question about life to my biological son Mark. Mark is a pediatrician, and author of a memoir entitled 'The Eden Express'. It is about his crack-up, straitjacket and padded cell stuff, from which he recovered sufficiently to graduate from Harvard Medical School.

Dr. Vonnegut said this to his doddering old dad: 'Father, we are here to help each other get through this thing, whatever it is.' So I pass that on to you. Write it down, and put it on your computer, so you can forget it.

I have to say that's a pretty good sound bite, almost as good as, 'Do unto others as you would have them do unto to you.' A lot of people think Jesus said that, because it is so much the sort of thing Jesus liked to say. But it was actually said by Confucius, a Chinese, five hundred years before there was that greatest and most humane of human beings, named Jesus Christ.

The Chinese also gave us, via Marco Polo, pasta and the formula for gunpowder. The Chinese were so dumb they only used gunpowder for fireworks.

And everybody was so dumb back then that nobody in either hemisphere even knew that there was another one.

We've sure come along way since then, only seven hundred years ago. Sometimes I wish we hadn't. I hate H-bombs and the Jerry Springer Show.

And while I have your attention, listen. Don't you think it's time we used DNA technology to find out who the freeloader is in the Tomb of the Unknown Soldier, so we can kick him out?

I love science. All humanists do. I'm particularly fond of the Big Bang Theory. It goes like this: There was once nothing, and it was so much nothing that there wasn't even such a thing as nothing. And then all of a sudden there was this great big BANG, and that's where all this crap came from. Forget the Bible.

Any questions?

You know what they should put over the entrance to the Physics Department? Just that one word:

BANG!

You know what else I think? I think life is no way to treat an animal, and not just people, but pigs and chickens, too. Life just hurts too much.

But to get back on to the subject of people like Confucius and Jesus and my son the doctor Mark, who've said how we could behave more humanely, and maybe make the world a less painful place. One of my favorites is Eugene Debs, from Terre Haute in my native state of Indiana. Please get a load of this:

Eugene Debs, who died back in 1926, when I was only four, ran several times as a Socialist candidate for President, if you can imagine such a ballot, had this to say while campaigning:

'As long as there is a lower class, I am in it. As long as there is a criminal element, I'm of it. As long as there is a soul in prison, I am not free.'

Doesn't anything Socialistic make you want to throw up? Like great public schools or health insurance for all?

How about Jesus's Sermon on the Mount, the Beatitudes?

Blessed are the meek, for they shall inherit the earth.

Blessed are the merciful, for they shall obtain mercy.
Blessed are the peacemakers, for they shall be called the children of God, and so on.

Not exactly planks in a Republican platform. Not exactly Donald Rumsfeld or Dick Cheney stuff.

For some reason, the most vocal Christians among us never mention the Beatitudes. But, often with tears in their eyes, they demand that the Ten Commandments be posted in public buildings. And of course that's Moses, not Jesus. I haven't heard one of them demand that The Sermon on the Mount, the Beatitudes, be posted anywhere.

'Blessed are the merciful' in a courtroom? 'Blessed are the peacemakers' in the Pentagon? Give me a break!

Who am I for in this next presidential election? I will vote for anybody, as long as he is a Nordic, heterosexual multi-millionaire, and went to Yale University, and was a member there of the secret society known as 'Skull and Bones'.

Only kidding, but seriously: there is a tragic flaw in our precious Constitution, and I don't know what can be done to fix it. This is it: Only nut cases want to be President.

This was true even in my high school. Only seriously disturbed people ran for Class President. We might have psychiatrists examine all candidates. But who but a nut case would want to be a psychiatrist?

But, when you stop to think about it, only a nut case would want to be a human being, if he or she had a choice. Such treacherous, untrustworthy, lying and greedy animals we are!

I wouldn't trust any one of you, no matter how friendly and innocent you may appear, any farther that I could throw you. Because you're human.

And for the love of God, as the Christians say, please don't trust me. I couldn't stand it.

My favourite song? It's 'How Could You Believe Me When I Said I Loved You, When You Know I've Been a Liar All My Life?'

You want to know what I pray every night?

I go down on my old knees, next to my cot in the coal bin, and I pray with all my heart, 'To whom it may concern. Couldn't you please put my soul inside a sea otter or barn owl instead?' I would rather be a sea otter than a human being, even if there has been another oil spill.

You want to know what the British mathematician and philosopher Bertrand Russell called this planet? He said it was 'the Lunatic Asylum of the Universe.' And he said the inmates had taken over, and we were tormenting each other and trashing the joint. And he wasn't talking about the germs or the elephants. He meant we the people.

Lord Russell lived to be almost a hundred. His dates are 1872 to 1970 AD. What does 'AD' signify? That commemorates an asylum inmate who was nailed to a wooden cross by a bunch of other inmates. With him still conscious, they, no kidding, hammered spikes through his wrists and insteps, and into the wood. Then they set the cross upright, so he had to dangle up there where even the shortest person in the crowd could see him writhing this way and that.

Can you imagine people doing such a thing to a person?

No problem. That's entertainment. Ask the devout Roman Catholic Mel Gibson, who as an act of piety, has just made a fortune with a movie about how Jesus was tortured. Never mind what Jesus said.

During the reign of King Henry the Eighth, founder of the Church of England, he had a counterfeiter boiled alive in public. Show biz again. Mel Gibson's next movie should be 'The Counterfeiter'. Box office records will again be broken.

One of the few good things about modern times is, if you die horribly on television, you will not have died in vain. You will have entertained us.

And what did the great British Historian Edward Gibbon have to say about the human record so far? He said, 'History is indeed little more than the register of the crimes, follies and misfortunes of mankind.'

The same can be said about this morning's issue of the *New York Times*.

Edward Gibbon's dates? 1737 to 1794 AD.

The French Algerian writer Albert Camus, who won a Nobel Prize for Literature in 1957, wrote that, 'There is but one truly serious philosophical problem, and that is suicide.'

So there's another barrel of laughs from literature.

Camus himself died in an automobile accident.

His dates? 1913 to 1960 AD.

Listen, all great literature is about what a bummer it is to be a human being: *Moby Dick, Huckleberry Finn, The Red Badge of Courage, the Iliad* and *the Odyssey, Crime and Punishment, The Bible* and *The Charge of the Light Brigade*.

But I have to say this in defence of humankind: No matter in what era in history, including the Garden if Eden, everybody just got there. And, except for the Garden of Eden, there were already all these crazy games going on, which could make you act crazy, even if you weren't crazy to begin with. Some of the games which were already going on when you got here were love and hate, Liberalism and Conservatism, automobiles and credit cards and girls' basketball.

On the subject of crazy games already going on before any of us ever got here:

If you keep up with current events in the supermarket tabloids, you know that a team of Martian anthropologists have been studying our culture for the past ten years, since our culture is the only one worth a nickel on the whole damn planet. You can forget Brazil and Argentina.

Anyway: They went back home last week, because they knew how terrible global warming was about to be. Their space vehicle wasn't a flying saucer. It was more like a flying soup tureen. And they're little all right, only six inches high. But they aren't green. They're mauve.

And their little mauve leader, by way of farewell, said in that teeny-weeny, tanny-wanny, toney-woney little voice of hers that there were two things about

American culture no Martian would ever understand.

'What is it,' she squeaked, 'what can it possibly be about blowjobs and golf?'

Even crazier than golf, though, is modern American politics where, thanks to TV, and for the convenience of TV, you can be only one of two kinds of human beings, either a Liberal or a Conservative.

Actually, this same sort of thing happened to the people of England ten generations ago, and Sir William Gilbert, of the radical team of Gilbert and Sullivan, wrote these words for a song about it back then:

I often think it's comical
How nature always does contrive
That every boy and every gal,
That's born into the world alive,
Is either a little Liberal,
Or a little Conservative.

Which one are you in this country, and it's practically a law of life that you have to be one or the other? If you aren't one or the other, you might as well be a doughnut.

If some of you still haven't decided, I'll make it easy for you.

If you want to take my guns away from me, and you're all for murdering fetuses, and love it when homosexuals marry each other, and want to give them kitchen showers, and you're for the poor, you're a Liberal.

If you are against those perversions and for the rich, you're a Conservative.

What could be simpler?

A show of hands, please: How many of you are Liberals?

On the subject of homosexuality: If you really want to hurt your parents, and you don't have the nerve to be gay, the least you can do is go into the arts. And in a few minutes I'll give a lesson in Creative Writing. That's what the blackboard is for.

In the meanwhile, though, I want to talk to you about our government's war on drugs. It's certainly a lot better than no drugs at all. It was illegal mescaline, which put my son Mark in the loony bin for a little while.

But get this: The two most widely abused and addictive and destructive of all substances are both perfectly legal. One, of course, is ethyl alcohol. And President George W. Bush, no less, and by his own admission, was smashed or tiddley-poo or four sheets to the wind a good deal of the time from when he was sixteen until he was forty-one. When he was forty-one, he says, Jesus appeared to him, and made him knock off the sauce, stop gargling nose paint.

Other drunks have seen pink elephants.

And what the heck, he doesn't make any of the big decisions, and couldn't, and wouldn't want to in any case.

All he has to do is say he will not cut and run, no matter what happens in Iraq or Afghanistan. Where in the heck can you cut and run to from Crawford, Texas? Dubuque, Iowa? Spokane?

And you know why I think he is so pissed off at Arabs? They invented algebra.

Arabs also invented the numbers we use, including a symbol for nothing, which nobody else had ever had before.

You think Arabs are dumb? Try doing long division with Roman numerals.

We're spreading democracy, are we? Same way European explorers brought Christianity to the Indians, what we now call 'Native Americans'. There's this story about Spaniards who were about to burn a Native American alive because he had been uppity in some way. And he was lashed to the stake, about to entertain, and a Spaniard tied a cross to the end of a long stick, and he held it up so the Native American could kiss it.

And the Native American asked why he should kiss it, and the Spaniard said if he kissed it he would go to Heaven. And the Native American asked if there were Spaniards in Heaven. He was told there were, and the Native American said he certainly didn't want to go there.

How ungrateful he was! How ungrateful are the people of Baghdad today.

So lets give another big tax cut to the super-rich. That'll teach Bin Laden a lesson he won't soon forget. Hail to the Chief.

That chief and his cohorts have as little to do with the Democracy as those Spaniards had to do with Jesus. We the people have absolutely no say in whatever they choose to do next. In case you haven't noticed, they've already cleaned out the treasury, passing it out to pals in the war and national security rackets, leaving your generation and the next one with a perfectly enormous debt, which you'll be asked to repay.

Nobody let out a peep when they did that to you, because big money and TV have disconnected every burglar alarm in the Constitution: The House, the Senate, the Supreme Court and the FBI, and We the People.

About my own history of foreign substance abuse. By the God or whatever, I am not an alcoholic, largely a matter of genes. I take a couple of drinks now and then, and will do it again tonight. But two is my limit. No problem.

I am of course notoriously hooked on cigarettes. I keep hoping the things will kill me. A fire at one end and a fool at the other.

And I have been a coward about heroin and cocaine and LSD and so on, afraid they might put me over the edge, and, unlike my son Mark, I might never come back again. I did smoke a joint of marijuana one time with Jerry Garcia of the Grateful Dead, just to be sociable. It didn't seem to do anything to me one way or the other, so I never did it again.

But I'll tell you one thing: I had a high that not even crack cocaine could match. That was when I got my first driver's license! Look out world, here comes Kurt Vonnegut. I'm what a car is now. I'm a hundred horsepower now, which is eleven hundred manpower, so don't mess with me. Hya, Babe, you want a lift somewhere?

And my car back then, a Studebaker, as I recall, was powered, as are almost all means of transportation and other machinery today, and electric power plants and furnaces, by the most addictive and destructive drugs of all, which are fossil fuels, so easy to set afire.

When you got here, even when I got here, the industrialized world was already hopelessly hooked on fossil fuels, and very soon now there won't be any more of those. Cold turkey.

You've heard of 'crack babies'? Those are babies who come into the world already hooked on crack because their mothers were hooked on crack. Well, we are the fossil fuel babies.

As I speak, we are burning the last whiffs and drops and chunks of fossil fuels in a binge of thermodynamic whoopee. And while we do that, our waste products continue to make the air unbreathable and the water undrinkable, and more and more life forms are dying because of us.

This is a university, isn't it? Isn't it OK to tell young people the truth here? I mean this isn't like TV news, is it?

And here's what I think the truth is; we are all addicts of those fossil fuels in a state of denial, about to face cold turkey.

And like so many addicts about to face cold turkey, our leaders are now committing violent crimes to get what little is left of what we're hooked on.

But relax. I've got a joke that will dispel the gloom. It's another Martian joke. This is it, and no matter what, we've still got music and our sense of humor.

There's bad news and good news tonight, my friends. The bad news is the Martians have landed in New York City and are staying at the Waldorf Astoria.

The good news is they only eat homeless people and pee gasoline.

Put some of that pee in a Ferrari, and you can go a hundred miles an hour. If you're a guy, you can have babes like you can't believe. Put some in a plane and you can go as fast as a bullet, and drop all kinds of crap on the Arabs below. Put some in a school bus and you can get the kids to and from school. Put some in a fire engine, and it will get firemen to a fire, so they can put the fire out. Put some in a Honda, and it'll get you to work, and then back home again.

And wait till you hear what the Martians poop. It's Uranium. Just one of them can light and heat every home and school and church and business in Tacoma.

What's it like to be my age? I can't parallel park worth a damn anymore, so please don't watch me while I try to do it. And gravity has become a lot less friendly and manageable than it used to be.

I have also become a flaming neuter. I'm as celibate as fifty per cent of the heterosexual Roman Catholic clergy. And celibacy is no root canal. It's so cheap and convenient. You don't have to do or say anything afterwards, because there is no afterwards.

And when my tantrun, which is what I call my TV set, flashes boobs and smiles in my face, and says everyone but me is going to get laid tonight, and this is a national emergency, so I've got to rush out and buy a car or pills, or a folding gymnasium I can hide under my bed, I laugh like a hyena. I know and you know that millions and millions of good Americans, present company not excepted, are not going to get laid tonight.

And we flaming neuters vote! So I am looking forward to the day when the

President of the United States, no less, who probably isn't going to get laid that night, declares a National Neuter Pride Day. And out of our closets we'll come by the millions. Shoulders squared, chins held high, we'll go marching up Main Streets all over this boob-crazed democracy of ours, and laughing like hyenas.

But hey, listen; I got a letter from a sappy woman a while back. She knew I was sappy too, a Franklin Roosevelt Democrat, a friend of the working stiffs. She was about to have a baby, not mine. She wanted to know if it was a mistake to bring an innocent little baby into a world as awful as this one is. I told her that what made life almost worth living for me was the saints I met. These were people who behaved compassionately and capably, no matter what, and they could be anywhere.

So maybe some of you tonight are or may become saints for her child to meet. Most of us are loaded with Original Sin. But a surprising number of us, not me, God knows, are loaded with Original Virtue. Ain't that sweet.

So now it's time for me to teach creative writing.

First rule: Don't use semicolons. They are transvestite hermaphrodites, representing nothing. All they do is show you've been to college.

And I realize that some of you may have trouble deciding whether I'm kidding or not. So from now on I will thumb my nose at you like when I'm kidding.

For instance? Join the National Guard or the Marines and teach Democracy. (*Nose*)

If I give you the finger, (*Finger*) it means Spokane is about to be attacked by Al Qaeda. In that case wave flags, if you have them. That always seems to scare them away. Please don't get the two signals mixed up, or you might accidentally start World War Three.

*Creative writing lesson on blackboard
followed by 'Blue Danube' on the P.A.*

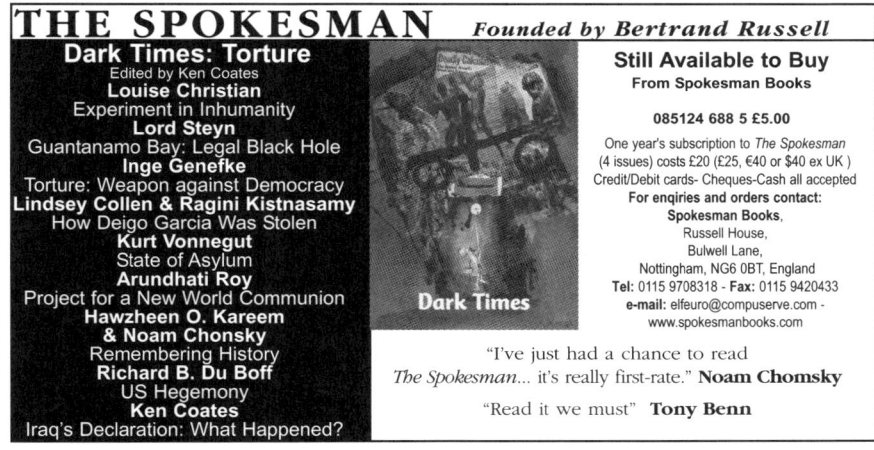

> Apr 22 - 04
>
> I AM FREE
>
> I AM HAPPY
>
> Peace
> Thank you.
> Mordechai Vanunu

Written in the garden of St. George's Cathedral, Jerusalem, on the afternoon of Thursday 22 April 2004.

Vanunu – Free at Last

Bruce Kent

Bruce Kent went to Ashkelon with a group of other campaigners to greet Mordechai Vanunu on his release from prison. He works with the Movement for the Abolition of War (www.abolishwar.org.uk).

The afternoon of Thursday 22 April was unreal. A few of Mordechai Vanunu's supporters, including his indefatigable brother, Meir, were sitting together with him in the sunshine in the garden of St George's Cathedral, Jerusalem, chatting and cracking pistachio nuts. Only the day before he had been released from prison after 18 years, 11 of which were spent in absolute solitary confinement.

Mordechai, now 49, spoke with dignity and even a sense of humour. I well remember receiving letters from him with lots of little holes cut out by the censor. The offending words were usually 'nuclear'. One day we received, to our surprise, a letter with all the offending cut-out pieces enclosed. Reminded of this, Vanunu laughed. He had once managed to distract the guard so that instead of putting them in the bin he had managed to enclose the deletions in the letter itself.

During those 18 years many of his supporters worried that he might suffer permanent mental disorientation: for two years the light in his cell was left on permanently. But this small man sitting in front of us and asking his own questions – 'How old are you, Bruce Kent?'– was calm and entirely sane. Nevertheless, he is deeply disappointed that after serving his whole sentence he is still not free to leave the country.

That was Thursday. The day before, the atmosphere outside the prison in Ashkelon when he was released had been anything but calm. More than 150 supporters, some from Israel but the majority from other countries, had gathered by 8 a.m. They came from Britain, the United States, Japan, Hungary, Poland, Canada, Ireland, Norway and the Netherlands. From Minnesota came Nick and Mary Eoloff, the American couple who adopted Vanunu some years ago and who have visited him many times since. The actress Susan York was the best-known British representative, but we also had with us Jeremy Corbyn MP (Labour) and Colin Breed MP (Lib Dem), as well as the distinguished human rights lawyer Benedict Birnberg. Well rehearsed in non-violence by the American Catholic Worker contingent, we stood dutifully behind the police barrier and held up our welcoming posters.

We were not alone. Numbers of very hostile people turned up. 'Traitor' was one of their more polite words. References to our parentage were made and posters of Vanunu were set on fire. Eggs splattered on a few backs.

As the release time approached, the tension increased and the number of cameras and microphones multiplied. The angry protesters were allowed close to the prison gates, with the police apparently outnumbered. Eventually some sort of cordon was organised. Since one Israeli newspaper had openly speculated on the possibility of someone shooting Vanunu, there was a certain anxiety. Finally we could see that inside the courtyard some sort of press conference was going on. Then, to mixed cheers and angry screams, Vanunu appeared at the gate, gave a victory sign, was bundled into a car, and driven off at high speed with a police escort. As an exercise in damage limitation by the Israeli authorities it was all a disaster.

The Defence Ministry security chief, Yehiel Horev, has been publicly criticised for his handling of the release. Already some of the restrictions imposed on Vanunu's activity are proving to be unworkable and are being interpreted in different ways by different authorities. There is nowhere in Israel where Vanunu can now live in security – let alone peace – given the hostility of the Zionist hard right. Yet it can do Israel no good whatsoever if Vanunu is attacked. Israelis might not like it, but the best way to cut its present losses would be to give Vanunu a passport and get him out of the country. Meanwhile, the courage of the Anglican Bishop of Jerusalem, Riah Abu el-Assal, in giving Vanunu sanctuary in St George's, deserves high praise. Vanunu is in serious danger.

Why this hostility? It is true that he broke his terms of employment when, in 1986, he revealed details to the *Sunday Times* about the Dimona nuclear plant and Israel's nuclear weapons programme. He had worked in the plant from 1976 to 1985. But sometimes moral obligations supersede legal ones. In Britain, Katherine Gunn and Clive Ponting both broke their civil service obligations for reasons of conscience and received public support for what they did. In his poem, 'I am your Spy', written in prison, Vanunu admits; 'I signed a form. Only now am I reading the rest of it.'

But there is much more to the hostility that this. Some of it relates to his conversion to Christianity, in Australia in 1986. One of the popular papers even had a picture of Vanunu, taken on the day of his release, flanked on both sides by clergymen in collars with a large headline over the whole story: 'Vanunu the Christian'. (Perhaps Israel is more accustomed to supportive rather than to critical Christians. The Baptist president of the United Christian Council in Israel, far from commenting on the 18 years and the ill treatment, could only say that Vanunu's bitterness and anger made him 'very pitiful'.)

Vanunu is also hated because, on the issue of Israel itself, he is clearly out of step with the Israeli majority; he has made it clear that he does not believe in a Jewish but a unitary state, where Jews and Palestinians coexist. 'Some of those who have turned Vanunu in to a hero are idealists who want to see a world free of nuclear weapons,' the *Jerusalem Post* commented on 20 April. 'Others seek to exploit this issue to weaken Israel as part of their battle against the Jewish State.'

It is a curious argument. A state without nuclear weapons might want to pretend it had them in order to appear stronger than it is. But a state with nuclear weapons, according to standard deterrence theory, ought actually to be more secure if everybody knows that it has them. Vanunu – if one believes in deterrence – has therefore in fact increased Israel's security.

In fact, Israel cherishes official ambiguity because its major ally, the United States, wants it that way. There has been an American commitment since 1969 to avoid putting pressure on Israel on the nuclear weapons issue as long as Israel promises to continue with its ambiguous nuclear façade. This long-standing commitment was reaffirmed by President Bill Clinton and Prime Minister Benjamin Netanyahu. To be open about the possession of nuclear weapons is to risk a legal challenge from within the United States to the massive American funding without which Israel would not survive in its present form.

The accusation that Vanunu has yet to reveal secrets about Dimona which could be relevant today is simply nonsense. He was never in a senior position at the plant, and it is now nineteen years since he worked there. In two decades nuclear weapons technology has moved on a long way. Dr Frank Barnaby, once director of the Stockholm International Peace Research Institute, has made this point repeatedly.

What Vanunu could tell the world about are the details of his 1986 kidnapping. That might be a mild embarrassment to the British and Italian governments since that conspiracy started in Britain and was completed in Italy, and no prosecutions have ever been attempted. It would hardly embarrass Israel, which takes some pride in the exploits of Mossad, its secret service.

For everyone else, Vanunu is one of the heroes of the age. His position has always been that nuclear weapons, not only those of Israel, should be eliminated and that there should be a democratic participation in the process of making that happen. In Israel the first parliamentary debate about its nuclear weapons programme in more than 35 years took place in 2000, and then only after an appeal to the Supreme Court. It lasted 52 minutes. Vanunu, at great cost to himself, has tried to lift the lid from a state secret. The editor of the *Sunday Times* said categorically that Vanunu neither asked for nor received financial reward.

His release comes at a moment of opportunity. In the spring of 2005 there will take place in New York what may possibly be the last review conference of the 1968 Nuclear Non-Proliferation Treaty. If there are no positive results, the treaty may as well go in the dustbin of history. Despite its title, it is a treaty not just about proliferation, but also about the abolition of nuclear weapons.

This requirement is now even stronger since, in 1996, the International Court of Justice ruled that, 'there exists an obligation to pursue in good faith and bring to conclusion negotiations leading to nuclear disarmament in all its aspects under strict and effective international control.' A draft treaty already exists covering all aspects of this process, including inspection and verification. Next year offers what may be a last chance. Today at least eight countries possess nuclear weapons and non-state organisations may well be trying to get their own. The list of nuclear accidents and miscalculations grows longer and longer as the history of the past 50 years is revealed. It is time to move from the reduction in numbers of nuclear weapons to nuclear weapons elimination.

Which is why I have a strong sympathy for the Israeli position. Were I a citizen of that country I would want to ask, 'why start with us?' It is, indeed, the five major nuclear weapons states that have led the way and it is for them to put the process in reverse. 'Do as I say not as I do' has never been a sound ethical position. Tony Blair could regain some of his lost credibility were he to come to the 2005 Non-Proliferation meeting with a promise to start abolition negotiations.

With grateful acknowledgements to The Tablet, 1 May 2004.

* * *

At the meeting of the European Network for Peace and Human Rights at the European Parliament in Brussels on 29/30 April 2004, the following communiqué was approved endorsing Mordechai Vanunu's appeal to Mohamed ElBaradei to inspect the Dimona facility.

We the undersigned participants in European Network for Peace and Human Rights endorse this statement:

1. We welcome the release of Mordechai Vanunu after 17-and-a-half years of wrongful imprisonment in Shikma prison in Ashkelon, following his kidnapping by Israeli agents;
2. We unreservedly condemn the new decision of the Israeli authorities henceforth to restrict Mr Vanunu's freedom of movement, to bar him from leaving the country, to limit his freedom of association, and to prevent him from meeting visitors from abroad or representatives of the media, to tap his telephone and to subject him to close surveillance;
3. We strongly support Mr Vanunu's call to remove all nuclear weapons from the Middle East. As he says in relation to Israeli nuclear weapons: 'Israel doesn't need nuclear arms, especially now that all the Middle East is free from nuclear arms…my message today to all the world is open the Dimona reactor for inspections. Call Mohamed ElBaradei [the International Atomic Energy Agency chief] to come and inspect the reactor.'
4. We recall the repeated demands at the United Nations General Assembly since 1987 for a nuclear-weapons free zone throughout the Middle East.
5. We believe that the existence of a developed nuclear arsenal in Israel shows how one-sided and specious are the calls of some powers for 'counter-proliferation', as distinct from 'non-proliferation'. No attempt has ever been made to persuade Israel, leave alone compel it, to forego nuclear weapons.
6. The case for a nuclear-weapon-free zone in the whole of the Middle East has always rested on the voluntary consent of the parties. It remains as strong as ever.

THE BERTRAND RUSSELL PEACE FOUNDATION
PEACE DOSSIER

2004   Number 11

ABUSE, ASSAULT AND MURDER OF PRISONERS IN IRAQ

On 26 February 2004 in Baghdad, the representatives of the International Committee of the Red Cross met with US Ambassador Paul Bremer, the head of the Coalition Provisional Authority, and the legal adviser to the United Kingdom's Special Representative in Iraq, Sir Jeremy Greenstock. Their task was to present a new Report which was the culmination of a series of earlier reports detailing alleged abuse of prisoners that dated back to April 2003, shortly after the invasion of Iraq was launched. The International Committee of the Red Cross is mandated by international agreement to monitor the full application of the Geneva Conventions regarding the treatment of persons deprived of their liberty. The Committee's 24-page report (reproduced below) detailed serial transgressions of the Conventions on the part of the Coalition Forces in Iraq during the arrest, internment and interrogation of persons deprived of their liberty. It spelt out which articles of the Conventions were being broken, and what the Coalition Forces and their Governments had to do to come back into compliance. The Report cites assaults and even the killing of persons who have been arrested, and the systematic abuse, amounting to torture, of special categories of detainees. (The normal usage of the Report refers to 'Coalition Forces', seldom distinguishing between their origins.) What was the response of the British Government to these grave charges? How did its law officers assess the reported transgressions of the Geneva Conventions? What did Ministers do to correct the catalogue of wrongdoing reported by the Red Cross, as a result of its 29 visits to 14 internment facilities in central and southern Iraq between March and November 2003? Questioned by the BBC on the Today programme (20 May 2004), Sir Jeremy Greenstock represented these events in a slightly different light:

Greenstock: '...My legal adviser attended the meeting between the Red Cross and Ambassador Bremer, and made sure that the passages about the British actions were sent straight back to the Ministry of Defence. But the Red Cross never drew my attention personally to the passages about American abuse and I was not aware of it.

    BBC: So the references to British abuse went straight to the MoD, and you had every reason to assume to a ministerial desk?

Greenstock: Yes, it went on the military net. We passed them across to our military colleagues in Baghdad, and we assumed that they were being dealt with, and in fact, as I understand, they were being dealt with… I'm talking about the end of February, into March.'

Whatever the Ministry of Defence did with Sir Jeremy's messages, they allegedly did not penetrate to members of the British Government. Adam Ingram, Minister for the Armed Forces, told the House of Commons on 4 May 2004:

'To date, I have received no such reports, but some may be in the process of being compiled.'

The Minister of Defence, Geoff Hoon, embroidered this answer, without throwing any further light on the question, on 10 May 2004:

'The interim ICRC report was not seen by Ministers until very recently. That is because it was an interim report to Ambassador Bremer, passed to the United Kingdom in strict confidence.'

In fact, there is no evidence that it was an interim report. Rather, it was a full and 'culminating' report, handed to both Bremer and Greenstock's representatives acting on behalf of the Coalition authorities. Hoon continued:

'…. The report to Ambassador Bremer was passed to Sir Jeremy Greenstock, then to the military representative in Iraq, and from there to the Permanent Joint Headquarters..'

As might be expected, Hoon's account of events appears to diverge from that of the Prime Minister's Official Spokesman, given below.

With greater candour, the Foreign Secretary returned to the Red Cross Report in the House of Commons the following day:

'With the benefit of hindsight it should have been made available to ministers but as it happens it was not.'

The Prime Minister did not address the question of the Red Cross report until 12 May:

'I first saw it on Monday. I did not know of the allegations in the report at the time... The report was not passed to Ministers in February.'

Clearly aware of the confusing impressions given by assorted Ministers, the No.10 apparatus arranged for a press briefing the day before the Prime Minister answered questions in the House:

'Asked to clarify whether Sir Jeremy Greenstock had seen the ICRC report, the Prime Minister's Official Spokesman (PMOS) said a meeting had been held when ICRC personnel had presented their report to Paul Bremer and British representatives, including Sir Jeremy's legal advisers. As a result of that meeting, the report had been sent to the relevant people in Iraq to be dealt with. It was important for people to recognise that its contents were already being acted on, which was why it had been handled in the way that it had. Confusion had arisen because we had thought that Sir Jeremy himself had read the report, when it fact

> '...the single most iconic image to come out of the abuse scandal – that of a hooded man standing naked on a box, arms outspread, with wires dangling from his fingers, toes and penis – may do a lot to undercut the administration's case that this was the work of a few criminal MPs. That's because the practice shown in that photo is an arcane torture method known only to veterans of the interrogation trade. "Was that something that [an MP] dreamed up by herself? Think again," says Darius Rejali, an expert on the use of torture by democracies. "That's a standard torture. It's called 'the Vietnam.' But it's not common knowledge. Ordinary American soldiers did this, but someone taught them."
>
> Who might have taught them? Almost certainly it was their superiors up the line. Some of the images from Abu Ghraib, like those of naked prisoners terrified by attack dogs or humiliated before grinning female guards, actually portray "stress and duress" techniques officially approved at the highest levels of the government for use against terrorist suspects. It is unlikely that President George W. Bush or senior officials ever knew of these specific techniques, and late last week Defense spokesman Larry Di Rita said that "no responsible official of the Department of Defense approved any program that could conceivably have been intended to result in such abuses." But a NEWSWEEK investigation shows that, as a means of pre-empting a repeat of 9/11, Bush, along with Defense Secretary Rumsfeld and Attorney General John Ashcroft, signed off on a secret system of detention and interrogation that opened the door to such methods. It was an approach that they adopted to sidestep the historical safeguards of the Geneva Conventions, which protect the rights of detainees and prisoners of war. In doing so, they overrode the objections of Secretary of State Colin Powell and America's top military lawyers – and they left underlings to sweat the details of what actually happened to prisoners in these lawless places.'
> *Newsweek investigation by John Barry and others, 24 May 2004*

he hadn't. Asked if Sir Jeremy had notified Downing Street of the mistake, the spokesman said no. It had become apparent that there was a discrepancy between what the Defence Secretary had said yesterday and what the Foreign Secretary had said today. Yes, it was a slight mistake, but it did not change the substance of the matter one iota. Asked how the error had come to light, the spokesman said that as he understood it, a member of the Opposition had spotted the discrepancy today and had pointed it out. Asked at what stage Sir Jeremy had finally found out about the ICRC report, the spokesman said that Sir Jeremy had always been aware of the report. He underlined the fact that it had not contained any new allegations about British troops that were not already being dealt with. That was why Ministers had not been informed of it. Put to him that Sir Jeremy would surely had warned the Prime Minister about it, the spokesman said that he was not aware of any such conversations.

Asked repeatedly if anyone had been aware of the substance of the allegations made by the Red Cross apart from Sir Jeremy Greenstock's legal advisers and officials in London who had received the report from Sir Jeremy's office, the spokesman pointed out that the Red Cross tended to deal with one country at a time when drafting reports. Both President Bush and the Prime Minister had made clear their shared view about the mistreatment of prisoners. It was for other Governments to deal with Red Cross reports relating to their own troops. Put to him that the ICRC's interim report in February had talked about 'Coalition Forces', the spokesman pointed out that the report had been presented to the Coalition Provisional Authority, not to the British Government. Officials had been asked by the CPA to deal with those concerns pertaining to British troops, which was precisely what they had done.

Asked if officials had been given a full copy of the ICRC report containing allegations about US troops as well as British forces, the spokesman said that officials had seen the report and had dealt with those concerns relating to British troops. Asked what British officials had known about other allegations, the spokesman said that the confidentiality under which the Red Cross operated meant that officials had responded in the way they had. The report was therefore a matter for the Red Cross. Asked if he was suggesting that Sir Jeremy Greenstock's legal advisers had decided not to pass on the concerns about US troops raised by the ICRC in their report because the Red Cross considered the confidential terms of their *modus operandi* as sacrosanct, the spokesman said that the officials had acted on their understanding of the Red Cross's very strict rules. We would welcome the publication of the ICRC's February and April reports. However, we had to abide by the wishes of the Red Cross.

Put to him repeatedly that there would be no breach of confidence were British officials to ask US officials what measures were being taken to prevent the mistreatment of Iraqi prisoners in the light of the fact that both sides had seen the same report, the spokesman said that the Red Cross gave us information relating to the conduct of our detention centres and the people we had detained. It was our responsibility to act within the parameters set out by the Red Cross. Asked if he was suggesting that we had not known about the mistreatment of Iraqi prisoners by US troops, the spokesman said that he was simply setting out the terms under which we operated when dealing with the Red Cross. Put to him that it seemed ridiculous that the Coalition had gone into Iraq to stop the abuse and yet we were unable to do so all because of the Red Cross's commitment to confidentiality, the spokesman said that he was not a spokesman for the Red Cross. All he could do was explain the circumstances in which officials had found themselves. In answer to further questions, the spokesman took the opportunity to point out that action had been taken both by the British and the US as a result of the ICRC report. In the end that was what was most important. As the Prime Minister had underlined many times recently, the mistreatment of prisoners was wrong, was not to be condoned and was entirely counter-productive. That was the factual position.

Asked if the Prime Minister agreed with the Foreign Secretary's view that in hindsight it would have been better had Ministers been told about the report, the spokesman said that as he had said this morning, there were always lessons to be learned in Government, as the Foreign Secretary had articulated today. Both the Prime Minister and President Bush had condemned in completely unambiguous terms the mistreatment of any prisoner and had underlined that such things should not happen. It was also important for people to recognise that this was not something which characterised the entire Coalition Force in Iraq. The Coalition was there to stop abuse. As General Sir Mike Jackson had said when the allegations had first appeared, we welcomed any evidence of mistreatment so that it could be properly assessed and acted upon if necessary. That position had not changed.

Asked if the Prime Minister believed that the Arab world distinguished between the conduct of the different countries comprising the Coalition, the spokesman said that as he had told journalists repeatedly this morning and over the last two days, the Prime Minister in no way under-estimated the damage done by allegations of mistreatment. That was why he had made it plain to everyone that he believed it was important for prisoners to be treated properly.

Asked if any action had been taken to ensure that future Red Cross reports would be brought to the attention of Ministers, the spokesman said that obviously there would have to be a discussion about this matter. It was not up to the Government to decide whether ICRC reports could be published more widely.

Asked if the Prime Minister had been shocked to discover that US troops had been involved in the mistreatment of Iraqi prisoners or if he had known what was going on prior to publication of the allegations and pictures in the media, the spokesman said that allegations of mistreatment should not have come as a surprise to anyone, including the media, because of the well known case of the man who had unfortunately died in custody. Equally, the fact that investigations were taking place should not have come as any surprise because that had been confirmed. However, what Ministers had not known about was the Red Cross report – and that was the basis on which we had been answering questions. Asked if Ministers had known about the scale of the alleged abuse, the spokesman said that any allegations which had been made had been investigated, as you would expect. As the Prime Minister had made clear, such activity would not be tolerated. It was wrong and counter-productive. Asked if he was implying that the Prime Minister had known what US troops were up to before the press had got hold of the story, the spokesman cautioned journalists against putting words into his mouth. As he had said, it had been widely known that allegations of mistreatment had been made and that they were being investigated.

Asked repeatedly if the Prime Minister had been aware of allegations of torture and 'systemised humiliation' in the Abu Ghraib prison before the photos had appeared in the media, the spokesman said the Prime Minister had always made it clear that mistreatment of any kind was wrong. Pressed by BBC News 24 to stop treating journalists like idiots and answer the question, the spokesman said that he would never treat journalists like idiots. He was trying to answer questions politely, regardless of the way they were being asked. He thought that a bit of civility wouldn't go amiss. The answer to the question was that if the Prime Minister was aware of anything untoward, he would of course act accordingly. He had always made it clear that any mistreatment was wrong and counter-productive. It went without saying that these actions went against the values of the Coalition.

Asked when people would know that the Prime Minister was becoming a liability in the light of today's report in *The Guardian*, the spokesman said that as a Civil Servant he was unable to comment on party matters.'

'SERIOUS VIOLATIONS OF INTERNATIONAL HUMANITARIAN LAW'

The 'Report of the International Committee of the Red Cross (ICRC) on the treatment by the coalition forces of prisoners of war and other protected persons by the Geneva Conventions in Iraq during arrest, internment and interrogation' is dated February 2004.

Executive summary

In its 'Report on the Treatment by the Coalition Forces of Prisoners of War and other protected persons in lraq', the International Committee of the Red Cross (ICRC) draws the attention of the Coalition Forces (the CF) to a number of serious violations of International Humanitarian Law. These violations have been documented and sometimes observed while visiting prisoners of war, civilian internees and other protected persons by the Geneva Conventions (hereafter called persons deprived of their liberty when their status is not specifically mentioned) in Iraq between March and November 2003. During its visits to places of internment of the Coalition Forces, the International Committee of the Red Cross collected allegations during private interviews with persons deprived of their liberty relating to the treatment by the Coalition Forces of protected persons during their capture arrest, transfer, internment and interrogation.

The main violations, which are described in the ICRC report and presented confidentially to the Coalition Forces, include:

● Brutality against protected persons upon capture and initial custody, sometimes causing death or serious injury

● Absence of notification of arrest of persons deprived of their liberty to their families causing distress among persons deprived of their liberty and their families

● Physical or psychological coercion during interrogation to secure information

● Prolonged solitary confinement in cells devoid of daylight

● Excessive and disproportionate use of force against persons deprived of their liberty resulting in death or injury during their period of internment

Serious problems of conduct by the Coalition Forces affecting persons deprived of their liberty are also presented in the report:

● Seizure and confiscation of private belongings of persons deprived of their liberty

● Exposure of persons deprived of their liberty to dangerous tasks

● Holding persons deprived of their liberty in dangerous places where they are not protected from shelling

According to allegations collected by ICRC delegates during private interviews with persons deprived of their liberty, ill-treatment during capture was frequent. While certain circumstances might require defensive precautions and the use of force on the part of battle group units, the International Committee of the Red Cross collected allegations of ill-treatment following capture which took place in Baghdad, Basrah, Ramadi and Tikrit, indicating a consistent pattern with respect to times and places of brutal behavior during arrest. The repetition of such behavior by Coalition Forces appeared to go beyond the reasonable legitimate and proportional use of force required to apprehend suspects or restrain persons resisting arrest or capture, and seemed to reflect a usual *modus operandi* by certain Coalition Forces battle group units.

According to the allegations collected by the International Committee of the Red Cross, ill-treatment during interrogation was not systematic, except with regard to persons arrested in connection with suspected security offences or deemed to have an 'intelligence' value. In these cases, persons deprived of their liberty under supervision of the Military Intelligence were at high risk of being subjected to a variety of harsh treatments ranging from insults, threats and humiliations to both physical and psychological coercion, which in some cases was tantamount to torture, in order to force cooperation with their interrogators.

The International Committee of the Red Cross also started to document what appeared to be widespread abuse of power and ill-treatment by the Iraqi police which is under the responsibility of the Occupying Powers, including threats to hand over persons in their custody to the Coalition Forces so as to extort money from them, effective hand over of such persons to the custody of the Coalition Forces on allegedly fake accusations, or invoking Coalition Forces orders or instructions to mistreat persons deprived of their liberty during interrogation.

In the case of the 'High Value Detainees' held in Baghdad International Airport, their continued internment, several months after their arrest, in strict solitary confinement in cells devoid of sunlight for nearly 23 hours a day constituted a serious violation of the Third and Fourth Geneva Conventions.

The International Committee of the Red Cross was also concerned about the excessive and disproportionate use of force by some detaining authorities against persons deprived of their liberty involved during their internment during periods of unrest or escape attempts that caused death and serious injuries. The use of firearms against persons deprived of their liberty in circumstances where methods without using firearms could have yielded the same result could amount to a serious violation of International Humanitarian Law. The International Committee of the Red Cross reviewed a number of incidents of shootings of persons deprived of their liberty with live bullets, which have resulted In deaths or injuries during periods of unrest related to conditions of internment or escape attempts. Investigations initiated by the Coalition Forces into these incidents concluded that the use of firearms against persons deprived of their liberty was legitimate. However, non-lethal measures could have been used to obtain the same results and quell the demonstrations or neutralize persons deprived of their liberty trying to escape.

Since the beginning of the conflict, the International Committee of the Red Cross has regularly brought its concerns to the attention of the Coalition Forces. The observations in the present report are consistent with those made earlier on several occasions orally and in writing to the Coalition Forces throughout 2003. In spite of some improvements in the material conditions of internment, allegations of ill-treatment perpetrated by members of the Coalition Forces against persons deprived of their liberty continued to be collected by the International Committee of the Red Cross and thus suggested that the use of ill-treatment against persons deprived of their liberty went beyond exceptional cases and might be considered as a practice tolerated by the Coalition Forces.

The International Committee of the Red Cross report does not aim to be exhaustive with regard to breaches of International Humanitarian Law by the Coalition Forces in Iraq. Rather, it illustrates priority areas that warrant attention and corrective action on the part of Coalition Forces, in compliance with their International Humanitarian Law obligations.

Consequently the International Committee of the Red Cross asks the authorities of the Coalition Forces in Iraq:

- to respect at all times the human dignity, physical integrity and cultural sensitivity of the persons deprived of their liberty held under their control
- to set up a system of notifications of arrest to ensure quick and accurate transmission of information to the families of persons deprived of their liberty
- to prevent all forms of ill-treatment moral or physical coercion of persons deprived of their liberty in relation to interrogation
- to set up an internment regime which ensures the respect of the psychological integrity and human dignity of the persons deprived of their liberty
- to ensure that all persons deprived of their liberty are allowed sufficient time every day outside in the sunlight, and that they are allowed to move and exercise in the outside yard
- to define and apply regulations and sanctions compatible with International Humanitarian Law and to ensure that persons deprived of their liberty are fully informed upon arrival about such regulations and sanctions
- to thoroughly investigate violations of International Humanitarian Law in order to determine responsibilities and prosecute those found responsible for violations of International Humanitarian Law
- to ensure that battle group units arresting individuals and staff in charge of internment facilities receive adequate training enabling them to operate in a proper manner and fulfill their responsibilities as arresting authority without resorting to ill-treatment or making excessive use of force.

Introduction

The International Committee of the Red Cross is mandated by the High Contracting Parties to the Geneva Conventions to monitor the full application of and respect for the Third and Fourth Geneva Conventions regarding the treatment of persons deprived of their liberty. The International Committee of the Red Cross reminds the High Contracting Parties concerned, usually in a confidential way, of their humanitarian obligations under all four Geneva Conventions, in particular the Third and Fourth Geneva Conventions as far as the treatment of persons deprived of their liberty is concerned and under Protocol I of 1977 additional to the Geneva Conventions, confirmed and reaffirmed rules of customary law and universally acknowledged principles of humanity.

The information contained in this report is based on allegations collected by the International Committee of the Red Cross in private interviews with persons deprived of their liberty during its visits to places of internment of the Coalition Forces between March and November 2003. The allegations have been thoroughly revised in order to present this report as factually as possible. The report is also based on other accounts given either by fellow persons deprived of their liberty inside internment facilities or by family members. During this period, the International Committee of the Red Cross conducted some 29 visits in 74 internment facilities in the central and southern parts of the country. The testimonies were collected in Camp Cropper (Core Holding Area, Military Intelligence section, 'High Value Detainees' section); Al-Salihlyye, Tasferat anti Al-Russafa prisons; Abu Ghraib Correctional Facility (including Camp Vigilant and the 'Military Intelligence' section); Umm Qasr and Camp Bucca, as well as several temporary internment places such as Tallil Trans-shipment Place, Camp Condor, Amarah Camp and the Field Hospital in Shaibah,

The International Committee of the Red Cross conditions for visits to persons deprived of their liberty in internment facilities are common for all countries where the organization operates. They can be expressed as follows:

● The International Committee of the Red Cross must have access to all persons deprived of their liberty who come within its mandate in their place of internment
● The International Committee of the Red Cross must be able to talk freely and in private with the persons deprived of their liberty of its choice and to register their identity
● The International Committee of the Red Cross must be authorized to repeat its visits to the persons deprived of their liberty
● The International Committee of the Red Cross must be notified of arrests, transfers and releases by the detaining authorities

Each visit to persons deprived of their liberty is carried out in accordance with the International Committee of the Red Cross's working procedures expressed as follows:
● At the beginning of each visit, the ICRC delegates speak with the detaining authorities to present the International Committee of the Red Cross's mandate and the purpose of the visit as well as to obtain general information on

internment conditions, total of interned population and movements of persons deprived of their liberty (release, arrest, transfer, death, hospitalization).
- The ICRC delegates, accompanied by the detaining authorities tour the internment premises.
- The ICRC delegates hold private interviews with persons of their choice who are deprived of their liberty, with no time limit in a place freely chosen and if necessary register them.
- At the end of each visit, the delegates hold a final talk with the detaining authorities to inform them about the International Committee of the Red Cross's findings and recommendations.

The aim of the report is to present information collected by the International Committee of the Red Cross concerning the treatment of prisoners of war by the Coalition Forces, civilian internees and other protected persons deprived of their liberty during the process of arrest, transfer, internment and interrogation.

The main places of internment where mistreatment allegedly took place included battle group unit stations; the military intelligence sections of Camp Cropper and Abu Ghraib Correctional Facility; Al-Baghdadi, Heat Base and Habbania Camp in Ramadi governorate; Tikrit holding area (former Saddam Hussein Islamic School); a former train station in Al-Khaim, near the Syrian border, turned into a military base; the Ministry of Defence and Presidential Palace in Baghdad, the former *mukhabarat* office in Basrah, as well as several Iraqi police stations in Baghdad.

In most cases, the allegations of ill-treatment referred to acts that occurred prior to the internment of persons deprived of their liberty in regular internment facilities, while they were in the custody of arresting authorities or military and civilian intelligence personnel. When persons deprived of their liberty were transferred to regular internment facilities, such as those administered by the military police, where the behavior of guards was strictly supervised, ill-treatment of the type described in this report usually ceased. In these places, violations of provisions of International Humanitarian Law relating to the treatment of persons deprived of their liberty were a result of the generally poor standard of internment conditions (long term internment in unsuitable temporary facilities) or of the use of what appeared to be excessive force to quell unrest or to prevent attempted escapes.

Treatment during arrest

Protected persons interviewed by International Committee of the Red Cross delegates have described a fairly consistent pattern with respect to times and places of brutality by members of the Coalition Forces arresting them.

Arrests as described in these allegations tended to follow a pattern. Arresting authorities entered houses usually after dark, breaking down doors, waking up residents roughly, yelling orders, forcing family members into one room under military guard while searching the rest of the house and further breaking doors, cabinets and other property. They arrested suspects, tying their hands in the back with flexi-cuffs, hooding them, and taking them away. Sometimes they arrested all adult males present in a house, including elderly, handicapped or sick people. Treatment often included pushing people around, insulting, taking aim with rifles, punching and kicking and striking with rifles. Individuals were often led away in whatever they happened to be wearing at the time of arrest – sometimes in pyjamas or underwear – and were denied the opportunity to gather a few essential belongings, such as clothing, hygiene items, medicine or eyeglasses. Those who surrendered with a suitcase often had their belongings confiscated. In many cases personal belongings were seized during the arrest, with no receipt being issued (see below).

Certain Coalition Forces military intelligence officers told the International Committee of the Red Cross that in their estimate between 70% and 90% of the persons deprived of their liberty in Iraq had been arrested by mistake. They also attributed the brutality of some arrests to the lack of proper supervision of battle group units.

In accordance with provisions of International Humanitarian Law which oblige the Coalition Forces to treat prisoners of war and other protected persons humanely and to protect them against acts of violence, threats thereof, intimidation and insults (Art. 13, 14, 17, 87, Third Geneva Convention; Art 5, 27, 31,32, 33 Fourth Geneva Convention), the International Committee of the Red Cross asks the authorities of the Coalition Forces to respect at all times the human dignity, physical integrity and cultural sensitivity of the persons deprived of their liberty hold under their control. The ICRC also asks the authorities of Coalition Forces to ensure that battle group units arresting individuals receive adequate training enabling them to operate in a proper manner and fulfill their responsibilities without resorting to brutality or using excessive force.

Notification to families and information for arrestees

In almost all instances documented by the International Committee of the Red Cross, arresting authorities provided no information about who they were, where their base was located, nor did they explain the cause of arrest. Similarly, they rarely informed the arrestee or his family where he was being taken and for how long, resulting in the *de facto* 'disappearance' of the arrestee for weeks or even months until contact was finally made.

When arrests were made in the streets, along the roads, or at checkpoints, families were not informed about what had happened to the arrestees until they managed to trace them or received news about them through persons who had been deprived of their liberty but were later released, visiting family members of fellow persons deprived of their liberty, or ICRC Red Cross Messages. In the absence of a system to notify the families of the whereabouts of their arrested relatives, many were left without news for months, often fearing that their relatives unaccounted for were dead.

Nine months into the present conflict, there is still no satisfactorily functioning system of notification to the families of captured or arrested persons, even though hundreds of arrests continue to be carried out every week. While the main places of internment (Camp Bucca and Abu Ghraib) are part of a centralized notification system through the National Information Bureau (and their data are forwarded electronically to the International Committee of the Red Cross on a regular basis), other places of internment such as Mosul or Tikrit are not. Notifications from those places therefore depend solely on capture or internment cards as stipulated by the Third and Fourth Geneva Conventions,

Since March 2003 capture cards *have* often been filled out carelessly, resulting in unnecessary delays of several weeks or months before families were notified, and sometimes resulting in no notification at all. It is the responsibility of the detaining authority to see to it that each capture or internment card is carefully filled out so that the International Committee of the Red Cross is in a position to effectively deliver them to families The current system of General Information Centers, set up under the responsibility of the Humanitarian Assistance Coordination Centers, while an improvement, remains inadequate, as families outside the main towns do not have access to them, lists made available are not complete and often outdated, and do not reflect the frequent transfers from one place of internment to another. In the absence of a better alternative, the International Committee of the Red Cross's delivery of accurate capture cards remains the most reliable, prompt and effective system to notify the families, provided cards are property filled out.

The International Committee of the Red Cross has raised this issue repeatedly with the detaining authorities since March 2003, including at the highest level of the Coalition Forces in August 2003. Despite some improvement hundreds of families have had to wait anxiously for weeks and sometimes months before learning of the whereabouts of their arrested family members. Many families travel for weeks throughout the country from one place of internment to another in search of their relatives and often come to learn about their whereabouts informally (through released detainees) or when the person deprived of his liberty is released and returns home.

Similarly, transfers, cases of sickness at the time of arrest, deaths, escapes or repatriations continue to be notified only insufficiently or are not notified at all by the Coalition Forces to the families in spite of their obligation to do so under International Humanitarian Law.

In accordance with provisions of both the Third Geneva Convention (Art. 70, 122, 123) and the Fourth Geneva Convention (Art. 106, 136 137, 138, 140), the International Committee of the Red Cross reminds the Coalition Forces of their treaty-based obligation to notify promptly the families of all prisoners of war and other protected persons captured or arrested by them. Within one week, prisoners of war and civilian internees must be allowed to fill out capture or internment cards mentioning at the very least their capture/arrest, address (current place of detention/internment) and state of health. These cards must be forwarded as rapidly as possible and may not be delayed in any manner. As long as there is no centralized system of notifications of arrest set up by Coalition Forces, it is of paramount importance that these capture cards be filled out properly, so as to allow the International Committee of the Red Cross to transmit them rapidly to the concerned families.

The same obligation of notification to families of captured or arrested persons applies to transfers, cases of sickness, deaths. escapes and repatriation and identification of the dead of the adverse party. All these events must be notified to the International Committee of the Red Cross with the full details of the persons concerned, so as to allow the International Committee of the Red Cross to inform the concerned families (Art 120, 121, 122, 123 Third Geneva Convention; Art. 129,130, 136, 137, 140 Fourth Geneva Convention).

Treatment during transfer and initial custody

The International Committee of the Red Cross collected several allegations indicating that following arrest persons deprived of their liberty were ill-treated, sometimes during transfer from their place of arrest to their initial internment facility. This ill-treatment would normally stop by the time the persons reached a regular internment facility, such as Camp Cropper, Camp Bucca or Abu Ghraib. The International Committee of the Red Cross also collected one allegation of death resulting from harsh conditions of interment and ill-treatment during initial custody.

One allegation collected by the International Committee of the Red Cross concerned the arrest of nine men by the Coalition Forces in a hotel in Basrah on 13 September 2003. Following their arrest, the nine men were made to kneel, face and hands against the ground, as if in a prayer position. The soldiers stamped on the back of the neck of those raising their head. They confiscated their money without issuing a receipt. The suspects were taken to Al-Hakimiya, a former office previously used by the *mukhabarat* in Basrah and then beaten severely by Coalition Forces personnel. One of the arrestees died following the ill-treatment, (name obscured, aged 28, married, father of two children). Prior to his death, his co-arrestees heard him screaming and asking for assistance.

The issued 'International Death Certificate' mentioned 'Cardio-respiratory arrest – asphyxia' as the condition directly leading to the death. As to the cause of that condition, it mentioned 'Unknown' and 'Refer to the coroner'. The certificate did not bear any other mention. An eyewitness description of the body given to the International Committee of the Red Cross mentioned a broken nose, several broken ribs and skin lesions on the face consistent with beatings. The father of the victim was informed of his death on 18 September, and was invited to identify the body of his son. On 3 October, the commander of the Coalition Forces in Basrah presented to him his condolences and informed him that an investigation had been launched and that those responsible would be punished. Two other persons deprived of their liberty were hospitalised with severe injuries. Similarly, a week later, an International Committee of the Red Cross medical doctor examined them in the hospital and observed large haematomas with dried scabs on the abdomen, buttocks, sides, thigh, wrists, nose and forehead consistent with their accounts of beatings received.

During a visit of the International Committee of the Red Cross in Camp Bucca [near Umm Qasr in southern Iraq] on 22 September 2003, a 61-year old person deprived of his liberty alleged that he had been tied, hooded and forced to sit on the hot surface of what he surmised to be the engine of a vehicle, which had caused severe burns to his buttocks. The victim had lost consciousness. The International Committee of the Red Cross observed large crusted lesions consistent with his allegations.

The International Committee of the Red Cross examined another person deprived of his liberty in the 'High Value Detainees' section in October 2003 who had been subjected to a similar treatment. He had been hooded, handcuffed in the back, and made to lie face down on a hot surface during transportation. This had caused severe skin burns that required three months hospitalisation. At the time of the interview he had been recently discharged from hospital. He had to undergo several skin grafts, the amputation of his right index finger, and suffered the permanent loss of the use of his left fifth finger secondary to burn-induced skin retraction. He also suffered extensive burns over the abdomen, anterior aspects of the lower extremities, the palm of his right hand and the sole of his left foot. The International Committee of the Red Cross recommended to the Coalition Forces that the case be investigated to determine the cause and circumstances of the injuries and the authority responsible for the ill-treatment. At the time of writing the results of the report were still pending.

During transportation following arrest, persons deprived of their liberty were almost always hooded and tightly restrained with flexi-cuffs. They were occasionally haematoma and linear marks compatible with repeated whipping or beating. He had wrist marks compatible with tight flexi-cuffs.

The International Committee of the Red Cross also collected allegations of deaths as a result of harsh internment conditions, ill-treatment, lack of medical attention, or the combination thereof, notably in Tikrit holding area formerly known as the Saddam Hussein Islamic School.

Some Coalition Forces military intelligence officers told the International Committee of the Red Cross that the widespread ill-treatment of persons deprived of their liberty during arrest, initial internment and 'tactical questioning' was due to a lack of military police on the ground to supervise and control the behavior and activities of the battle groups units, and the lack of experience of intelligence officers in charge of the 'tactical questioning'.

In accordance with provisions of International Humanitarian Law which oblige the Coalition Forces to treat prisoners of war and other protected persons humanely and to protect them against acts of violence, threats thereof, intimidation and insults (Art 13, 14,17, 87, Third Geneva Convention; Articles 5, 27, 31,32, 33 Fourth Geneva Convention), the International Committee of the Red Cross asks the authorities of the Coalition Forces to respect at all times the human dignity, physical integrity and cultural sensitivity of the persons deprived of their liberty held in Iraq under their control.

The International Committee of the Red Cross also asks the authorities of the Coalition Forces to ensure that battle group units transferring and/or holding individuals receive adequate training enabling them to operate in a proper manner and meet their responsibilities without resorting to brutality or using excessive force.

Treatment during interrogation

Arrests were usually followed by temporary internment at battle group level or at initial interrogation facilities managed by military intelligence personnel, but accessible to other intelligence personnel (especially in the case of security detainees). The ill-treatment by the Coalition Forces personnel during interrogation was not systematic, except with regard to persons arrested in connection with suspected security offences or deemed to have an 'intelligence' value. In these cases, persons deprived of their liberty supervised by the military intelligence were subjected to a variety of ill-treatments ranging from insults and humiliation to both physical and psychological coercion that in some cases might amount to torture in order to force them to cooperate with their interrogators. In certain cases, such as in Abu Ghraib military intelligence section, methods of physical and psychological coercion used by the interrogators appeared to be part of the standard operating procedures by military intelligence personnel to obtain confessions and extract information. Several military intelligence officers confirmed to the International Committee of the Red Cross that it was part of the military intelligence process to hold a person deprived of his liberty naked in a completely dark and empty cell for a prolonged period to use inhumane and degrading treatment, including physical and psychological coercion, against persons deprived of their liberty to secure their cooperation.

Methods of ill-treatment

The methods of ill-treatment most frequently alleged during interrogation included
● Hooding, used to prevent people from seeing and to disorient them, and also to prevent them from breathing freely. One or sometimes two bags, sometimes with an elastic blindfold over the eyes which, when slipped down, further impeded proper breathing. Hooding was sometimes used in conjunction with beatings thus increasing anxiety as to when blows would come. The practice of hooding also allowed the interrogators to remain anonymous and thus to act with impunity. Hooding could last for periods from a few hours to up to 2 to 4 consecutive days, during which hoods were lifted only for drinking, eating or going to the toilet;
● Handcuffing with flexi-cuffs, which were sometimes made so tight and used for such extended periods that they caused skin lesions and long-term after-effects on the hands (nerve damage), as observed by the International Committee of the Red Cross;
● Beatings with hard objects (including pistols and rifles), slapping, punching, kicking with knees or feet on various parts of the body (legs, sides, lower back, groin);

- Pressing the face to the ground with boots;
- Threats (of ill-treatment, reprisals against family members, imminent execution or transfer to *Guantanamo):*
- Being stripped naked for several days while held in solitary confinement in an empty and completely dark cell that included a latrine;
- Being held in solitary confinement combined with threats (to intern the individual indefinitely, to arrest other family members, to transfer the individual to Guantanamo), insufficient sleep, food or water deprivation, minimal access to showers (twice a week), denial of access to open air and prohibition of contacts with other persons deprived of their liberty;
- Being paraded naked outside cells in front of other persons deprived of their liberty, and guards, sometimes hooded or with women's underwear over the head;
- Acts of humiliation such as being made to stand naked against the wall of the cell with arms raised or with women's underwear over the head for prolonged periods – while being laughed at by guards, including female guards, and sometimes photographed in this position;
- Being attached repeatedly over several days, for several hours each time, with handcuffs to the bars of their cell door in humiliating (i.e. naked or in underwear) and/or uncomfortable position causing physical pain;
- Exposure while hooded to loud noise or music, prolonged exposure while hooded to the sun over several hours, including during the hottest time of the day when temperatures could reach 50 degrees Celsius (122 degrees Fahrenheit) or higher;
- Being forced to remain for prolonged periods in stress positions such as squatting or standing with or without the arms lifted.

These methods of physical and psychological coercion were used by the military intelligence in a systematic way to gain confessions and extract information or other forms of cooperation from persons who had been arrested in connection with suspected security offences or deemed to have an 'intelligence value'.

Military Intelligence section, 'Abu Ghraib Correctional Facility'

In mid-October 2003, the International Committee of the Red Cross visited persons deprived of their liberty undergoing interrogation by military intelligence officers in Unit lA, the 'isolation section' of 'Abu Ghraib' Correctional Facility. Most of these persons deprived of their liberty had been arrested in early October. During the visit, ICRC delegates directly witnessed and documented a variety of methods used to secure the cooperation of the persons deprived or their liberty with their interrogators. In particular they witnessed the practice of keeping persons deprived of their liberty completely naked in totally empty concrete cells and in total darkness allegedly for several consecutive days. Upon witnessing such cases, the International Committee of the Red Cross interrupted its visits and requested an explanation from the authorities. The military intelligence officer in charge of the interrogation explained that this practice was 'part of the process'. The process appeared to be a give-and-take policy whereby persons deprived of their liberty were 'drip-fed' with new items (clothing, bedding, hygiene articles, lit cell, etc.) in exchange for their 'cooperation'. The International Committee of the Red Cross also visited other persons deprived of their liberty held in total darkness, others in dimly lit cells who had been allowed to dress following periods during which they had been held naked. Several had been given women's underwear to wear under their jumpsuit (men's underwear was not distributed), which they felt to be humiliating.

The International Committee of the Red Cross documented other forms of ill-treatment, usually combined with those described above, including threats, insults, verbal violence, sleep deprivation caused by the playing of loud music or constant light in cells devoid of windows, tight handcuffing with flexi-cuffs causing lesions and wounds around the wrists. Punishment included being made to walk in the corridors handcuffed and naked, or with women's underwear on the head, or being handcuffed either dressed or naked to the bed bars or the cell door. Some persons deprived of their liberty presented physical marks and psychological symptoms which were compatible with these allegations. The International Committee of the Red Cross medical delegate examined persons deprived of their liberty presenting signs of concentration difficulties, memory problems, verbal expression difficulties, incoherent speech, acute anxiety reactions, abnormal behaviour and suicidal tendencies. These symptoms appeared to have been caused by the methods and duration of interrogation. One person held in isolation that the International Committee of the Red Cross examined was unresponsive to verbal and painful stimuli. His heart rate was 120 beats per minute and his respiratory rate 18 per minute. He was diagnosed as suffering from somatoform (mental) disorder, specifically a conversion disorder, most likely due to the ill-treatment he was subjected to during interrogation.

According to the allegations collected by the International Committee of the Red Cross, detaining authorities also continued to keep persons deprived of their liberty during the period of interrogation, uninformed of the reason for their arrest. They were often questioned without knowing what they were accused of. They were not allowed to ask questions and were not provided with an opportunity to seek clarification about the reason for their arrest. Their treatment tended to vary according to their degree of cooperation with their interrogators: those who cooperated were afforded preferential treatment such as being allowed contacts with other persons deprived of their liberty, being allowed to phone their families, being given clothes, bedding equipment. food, water or cigarettes, being allowed access to showers, being held in a lit cell, etc.

Umm Qasr and Camp Bucca

Since the establishment of Umm Qasr camp and its successor, Camp Bucca, persons deprived of their liberty undergoing interrogation, whether they had been arrested by British, Danish, Dutch or Italian armed forces were segregated from other internees in a separate section of the camp designed for investigation. This section was initially operated by the British Armed Forces who called it Joint Field Intelligence Team. On 7 April, its administration was handed over to the US Armed Forces, which renamed it Joint Interrogation Facility/Interrogation Control Element. On 25 September 2003, its administration was handed back to the British Armed Forces.

Coalition Forces intelligence personnel interrogated persons deprived of their liberty of concern to them in this section. They were either accused of attacks against the Coalition Forces or deemed to have an 'intelligence value'. They could be held there from a few days to several weeks, until their interrogation was completed. During a visit in September 2003, the International Committee of the Red Cross interviewed in that section several persons deprived of their liberty that had been held there for periods from three to four weeks.

Initially, inmates were routinely treated by their guards with general contempt, with petty violence such as having orders screamed at them and being cursed, kicked, struck with rifle butts, roughed up or pushed around. They were reportedly handcuffed in the back and hooded for the duration of the interrogation and were prohibited from talking to each other or to the guards. Hooding appeared to be motivated by security concerns as well as to be part of standard intimidation techniques used by military intelligence personnel to frighten inmates into cooperating. This was combined with deliberately maintaining uncertainty about what would happen to the inmates, and a generally hostile attitude on the part of the guards. Conditions of internment improved according to the degree of cooperation of the person deprived of his liberty. Interrogated persons deprived of their liberty were held in two separate sections. Those under initial investigation were reportedly not allowed to talk to each other (purportedly to avoid exchange of information and 'versions of events' between them). They were not allowed to stand up or walk out of the tent but they had access to water with which to wash themselves. Once they had cooperated with their interrogators, they were transferred to the 'privileged' tent where the above-mentioned restrictions were lifted.

Persons deprived of their liberty undergoing interrogation by the Coalition Forces were allegedly subjected to frequent cursing, insults and threats, both physical and verbal, such as having rifles aimed at them in a general way or directly against the temple, the back of the head, or the stomach, and threatened with transfer to Guantanamo, death or indefinite internment. Besides mentioning the general climate of intimidation maintained as one of the methods used to pressure persons deprived of their liberty to cooperate with their interrogators, none of those interviewed by the International Committee of the Red Cross in Umm Qasr and Camp Bucca spoke of physical ill-treatment during interrogation. All allegations of ill-treatment referred to the phase of arrest, initial internment (at collecting points, holding areas) and 'tactical questioning' by military intelligence officers attached to battle group units, prior to transfer to Camp Bucca.

Previous actions taken by the International Committee of the Red Cross in 2003 on the issue of treatment

On 1 April, the International Committee of the Red Cross informed orally the political advisor of the commander of British Armed Forces at the Coalition Forces Central Command in Doha about methods of ill-treatment used by military intelligence personnel to interrogate persons deprived of their liberty in the internment camp of Umm Qasr. This intervention had the immediate effect to stop the systematic use of hoods and flexi-cuffs in the interrogation section of Umm Qasr. Brutal treatment of persons deprived of their liberty also allegedly ceased when the 800th Military Police Brigade took over the guarding of that section in Umm Qasr. UK Forces handed over Umm Qasr holding area to the 800th Military Police Brigade on 09.04.03. The 800th Military Police Brigade then built Camp Bucca two kilometers away.

In May 2003, the International Committee of the Red Cross sent to the Coalition Forces a memorandum based on over 200 allegations of ill-treatment of prisoners of war during capture and interrogation at collecting points, battle group stations and temporary holding areas. The allegations were consistent with marks on bodies observed by the medical delegate. The memorandum was handed to [name obscured] US Central Command in Doha, State of Qatar. Subsequently, one improvement consisted in the removal of wristbands with the remark 'terrorist' given to foreign detainees.

In early July the International Committee of the Red Cross sent the Coalition Forces a working paper detailing approximately 50 allegations of ill-treatment in the military intelligence section of Camp Cropper, at Baghdad International Airport. They included a combination of petty and deliberate acts of violence aimed at securing the cooperation of the persons deprived of their liberty with their interrogators: threats (to intern individuals indefinitely, to arrest other family members, to transfer individuals to Guantanamo) against persons deprived of their liberty or against members of their families (in particular wives and daughters); hooding; tight handcuffing; use of stress positions (kneeling, squatting, standing with arms raised over the head) for three or four hours; taking aim at individuals with rifles, striking them with rifle butts, slaps, punches, prolonged exposure to the sun, and isolation in dark cells. International Committee of the Red Cross delegates witnessed marks on the bodies of several persons deprived of their liberty consistent with their allegations. In one illustrative case, a person deprived of his liberty arrested at home by the Coalition Forces on suspicion of involvement in an attack against the Coalition Forces was allegedly beaten during interrogation in a location in the vicinity of Camp Cropper. He alleged that he had been hooded and cuffed with flexi-cuffs, threatened to be tortured and killed, urinated on, kicked in the head, lower back and groin, force-fed a baseball which was tied into the mouth using a scarf and deprived of sleep for four consecutive days. Interrogators would allegedly take turns ill-treating him, When he said he would complain to the International

Committee of the Red Cross he was allegedly beaten more. An International Committee of the Red Cross medical examination revealed haematoma in the lower back, blood in urine, sensory loss in the right hand due to tight handcuffing with flexi-cuffs, and a broken rib.

Shortly after that intervention was sent, the military intelligence internment section was closed and persons deprived of their liberty were transferred to what became the 'High Value Detainees' section of the airport, a regular internment facility under the command of the 115th Military Police Battalion. From this time onwards, the International Committee of the Red Cross observed that the ill-treatment of this category of persons deprived of their liberty by military intelligence declined significantly and even stopped, while their interrogation continued through to the end of the year 2003.

Allegations of ill-treatment by Iraqi police

The International Committee of the Red Cross has also collected a growing body of allegations relating to widespread abuse of power and ill-treatment of persons in the custody of Iraqi police. This included the extensive practice of threatening to handover these persons to the Coalition Forces for internment, or claiming to act under the Coalition Forces' instructions, in order to abuse their power and extort money from persons taken in custody. Allegations collected by the International Committee of the Red Cross indicated that numerous people had been handed over to the Coalition Forces on the basis of unfounded accusations (of hostility against the Coalition Forces, or belonging to opposition forces) because they were unable or unwilling to pay bribes to the police. Alleged ill-treatment during arrest and transportation included hooding, tight handcuffing, verbal abuse, beating with fists and rifle butts, and kicking. During interrogation, the detaining authorities allegedly whipped persons deprived of their liberty with cables on the back, kicked them in the lower parts of the body, including in the testicles, handcuffed and left them hanging from the iron bars of the cell windows or doors in painful positions for several hours at a time, and burned them with cigarettes (signs on bodies witnessed by International Committee of the Red Cross delegates). Several persons deprived of their liberty alleged that they had been made to sign a statement that they had not been allowed to read. These allegations concerned several police stations in Baghdad including Al-Qana, Al-Jiran Al-Kubra in al-Amariyya, Al-Hurriyyeh in Al-Doura, Al-Salhiyye in Salhiyye, and Al-Baiah. Many persons deprived of their liberty drew parallels between police practices under the occupation with those of the former regime.

In early June 2003, for instance, a group of persons deprived of their liberty was taken to the former police academy after they had been arrested. There, they were allegedly hooded and cuffed and made to stand against a wall while a policeman placed his pistol against their heads and pulled the trigger in a mock execution (the pistol was in fact unloaded); they were also allegedly forced to sit on chairs where they were hit on the legs, the soles of their feet and on their sides with sticks They also allegedly had water poured on their legs and had electrical shocks administered to them with stripped tips of electric wires. The mother of one of the persons deprived of liberty was reportedly brought in and the policemen threatened to mistreat her. Another person deprived of his liberty was threatened with having his wife brought in and raped. They were made to fingerprint their alleged confessions of guilt, which resulted in their transfer to the Coalition Forces to be interned pending trial.

The International Committee of the Red Cross reminds the authorities of the Coalition Forces that prisoners of war and other protected persons in the custody of occupying forces must be humanely treated at all times: they must not be subjected to cruel or degrading treatment and must be protected against all acts of violence (Art. 13, 14, Third Geneva Convention; Art. 27, Fourth Geneva Convention). Torture and other forms of physical and psychological coercion against prisoners of war and other interned persons for the purpose of eliciting confession or information is prohibited in all cases and under all circumstances without exception (Art. 17 and 87, Third Geneva Convention; Art. 5, 31 and 32. Fourth Geneva Convention). Confessions extracted under coercion or torture can never be used as evidence of guilt (Art. 99, Third Geneva Convention, Art. 31, Fourth Geneva Convention). Such violations of International Humanitarian Law should be thoroughly investigated in order to determine responsibilities and prosecute those found responsible (Art. 129, Third Geneva Convention and Art. 146, Fourth Geneva Convention).

Treatment in regular internment facilities
General conditions of treatment

The International Committee of the Red Cross assessed the treatment of persons deprived of their liberty in regular internment facilities by Coalition Forces personnel as respectful with a few individual exceptions due to individual personalities or occasional loss of control on the part of the guards. Abusive behavior by guards, when reported to their officers, was usually quickly reprimanded and disciplined by superiors.

The International Committee of the Red Cross often noted a serious communication gap between detention personnel and persons deprived of their liberty, primarily due to the language barrier, which resulted in frequent misunderstandings. This was compounded by a widespread attitude of contempt on the part of guards, in reaction to which persons deprived of their liberty, who often complained of being treated like inferiors, adopted a similar attitude.

The International Committee of the Red Cross occasionally observed persons deprived of their liberty being slapped, roughed up, pushed around or pushed to the ground either because of poor communication (a failure to understand or a misunderstanding of orders given in English was construed by guards as resistance or disobedience), a disrespectful attitude on the part of guards, a reluctance by persons deprived of their liberty to comply with orders, or a loss of temper by guards.

Disciplinary measures included being taken out of the compound, handcuffed and made to stand, sit, squat or lie down in the sand under the sun for up to three or four hours, depending on the breach of discipline (disrespectful behavior towards guards, communication between persons deprived of their liberty transferring from one compound to another, disobeying orders); temporary suspension of cigarette distribution, and temporary segregation in disciplinary confinement sections of the detention facilities.

Despite the fact that reductions in the availability of water or food rations or, more commonly, cigarettes were occasionally observed, the prohibition on collective punishment provided far under International Humanitarian Law (Art. 26.6, 87.3, Third Geneva Convention and Art. 33, Fourth Geneva Convention) appeared to be generally respected by detaining authorities.

'High Value Detainees' section, Baghdad International Airport

Since June 2003, over a hundred 'high value detainees' have been held for nearly 23 hours a day in strict solitary confinement in small concrete cells devoid of daylight, This regime of complete isolation strictly prohibited any contact with other persons deprived of their liberty, guards, family members (except through Red Cross Messages) and the rest of the outside world. Even spouses and members of the same family were subject to this regime. Persons deprived of their liberty whose 'investigation' was nearing completion were reportedly allowed to exercise together outside their cells for twenty minutes twice a day or go to the showers or toilets together. The other persons deprived of their liberty still under interrogation reportedly continued to be interned in total 'segregation' (i.e. they were allowed to exercise outside their cells for twenty minutes twice a day and to go to the showers or toilets but always alone and without any contact with others). Most had been subjected to this regime for the past five months. Attempts to contact other persons deprived of their liberty or simply to exchange glances or greetings were reportedly sanctioned by reprimand or temporary deprivation of time outside their cells. Since August 2003, the detainees have been provided with the Koran. They have been allowed to receive books of a non-political nature, but no newspapers or magazines on current affairs. The internment regime appeared to be motivated by a combination of security concerns (isolation of the persons deprived of their liberty from the outside world) and the collection of intelligence. All had been undergoing interrogation since their internment in spite of the fact that none had been charged with criminal offence.

On 30 October 2003, the International Committee of the Red Cross wrote to the Detaining Authorities recommending that this policy be discontinued and replaced by a regime of internment consistent with the Coalition Force's obligations under the Geneva Conventions.

The internment of persons in solitary confinement for months at a time in cells devoid of daylight for nearly 23 hours a day is more severe than the forms of internment provided for in the Third and Fourth Geneva Conventions (investigation of criminal offences or disciplinary punishment). It cannot be used as a regular, ordinary mode of holding of prisoners of war or civilian internees. The International Committee of the Red Cross reminds the authorities of the Coalition Forces in Iraq that internment of this kind contravenes Articles 21, 25, 89, 90, 95, 103 of the Third Geneva Convention and Articles 27, 41, 42, 78, 82, 118, 125 of the Fourth Geneva Convention. The International Committee of the Red Cross recommends to the authorities of the Coalition Forces that they set up an internment regime which ensures respect for the psychological integrity and human dignity of the persons deprived of their liberty and that they make sure that all persons deprived of their liberty are allowed sufficient time every day outside in the sunlight and the opportunity to move about and exercise in the outside yard.

Excessive and disproportionate use of force against persons deprived of their liberty by the detaining authorities

Since March 2003, the International Committee of the Red Cross recorded, and in some cases witnessed, a number of incidents in which guards shot at persons deprived of their liberty with live ammunition, in the context either of unrest relating to internment conditions or of escape attempts by individuals:

Camp Cropper, 24 May 2003: In the context of a hunger strike, unrest broke out in the camp prior to the International Committee of the Red Cross visit. One person deprived of his liberty suffered a gunshot wound.

Camp Cropper, 9 June 2003: Six persons deprived of their liberty were injured by live ammunition after a guard opened fire on the group in an attempt to quell a demonstration.

Camp Cropper, 12 June 2003: Two, or possibly three, persons deprived of their liberty were shot at when they attempted to escape through the barbed wire fence. One of them, Akheel Abd Al-Hussein from Baghdad, was wounded and later died after being taken to the hospital. The other person deprived of his liberty was recaptured and received treatment for gunshot wounds.

Abu Ghraib, 13 June 2003: When unrest flared up, guards from three watchtowers opened fire at the demonstrators, injuring seven persons deprived of their liberty and killing another, Alaa Jasim Hassan. The authorities investigated the matter and concluded that the 'shooting was justified as the three tower [guards] determined that the lives of the interior guards were threatened'.

Abu Ghraib, late June 2003: During unrest, one person deprived of his liberty was injured by live ammunition when a guard opened fire.

Abu Ghraib, 24 November 2003: During a riot four detainees were killed by US Military Police guards. The killing took place after unrest erupted in one of the compounds (no 4). The detainees claimed to be unhappy with the situation of detention. Specifically, lack of food, clothing, but more importantly the lack of judicial guarantees and, especially important during the time of Eid al-Fitr, lack of family visits or lack of contacts altogether. The detainees alleged to have gathered near the gate whereupon the guards panicked and started shooting. Initially, non-lethal ammunition was used which was subsequently replaced by live ammunition.

The report handed over by the Coalition Forces to the International Committee of the Red Cross states that detainees were trying to force open the gate. It further states that several verbal warnings were given and non-lethal ammunition fired at the crowd. After 25 minutes deadly force was applied resulting in the death of four detainees [names obscured].

The narrative report furnished by the Coalition Forces does not address the reason for the riot in any way and does not give any recommendations as to how a similar incident could be avoided. It does not question the use of lethal force during such an incident.

Camp Bucca, 16-22 April 2003: International Committee of the Red Cross delegates witnessed a shooting incident which caused the death of one person deprived of his liberty and injury of another. A first shot was fired on the ground by a soldier located outside the compound in a bid to rescue one of the guards allegedly being threatened by a prisoner of war armed with a stick; the second shot injured a prisoner of war in the left forearm, and the third shot killed another prisoner of war.

Camp Bucca, 22 September 2003: Following unrest in a section of the camp, one person deprived of his liberty, allegedly throwing stones, was fired upon by a guard in a watchtower. He suffered a gunshot wound to the upper part of the chest, the bullet passed through the chest and exited form the back. The investigation undertaken by the Coalition Forces concluded that 'the compound guards correctly utilized the rules of engagement and that numerous non-lethal rounds were dispersed to no avail'. The person deprived of his liberty 'was the victim of a justifiable shooting'. An International Committee of the Red Cross delegate and an interpreter witnessed most of the events. At no point did the persons deprived of their liberty, and the victim shot at, appear to pose a serious threat to the life or security of the guards who could have responded to the situation with less brutal measures. The shooting showed a clear disregard for human life and security of the persons deprived of their liberty.

These incidents were investigated summarily by the Coalition Forces. They concluded in all cases that a legitimate use of firearms had been made against persons deprived of their liberty, who, except perhaps in Abu Ghraib on 13 June 2003, were unarmed and did not appear to pose any serious threat to anyone's life justifying the use of firearms. In all cases, less extreme measures could have been used to quell the demonstrations or neutralize persons deprived of their liberty trying to escape.

In connection with the 22 September 2003 incident, the International Committee of the Red Cross wrote on 23 October to the Commander of the 800th MP Brigade and recommended the adoption of crowd control measures consistent with the rules and principles of the Third and Fourth Geneva Conventions and other applicable international norms relating to the use of force or firearms by law-enforcement personnel.

Since May 2003, the International Committee of the Red Cross repeatedly recommended to the Coalition Forces to use non-lethal methods to deal with demonstrations, riots or escape attempts. In Camp Cropper, its recommendations were heeded. After initial deplorable incidents no further shooting of persons deprived of their liberty has occurred since November 2003. In mid-July, the International Committee of the Red Cross witnessed a demonstration in that camp: in spite of some violence by the persons deprived of their liberty, the problem was efficiently dealt with by the camp commander without any excessive use of force. He called in anti-riot military policemen, refrained from any act that might have provoked further anger from the persons deprived of their liberty, waited patiently for the emotions to calm down and then sought to establish dialogue with the persons deprived of their liberty though their section representatives. The unrest was quieted down without any violence.

The International Committee of the Red Cross reminds the authorities of the Coalition Forces that the use of firearms against persons deprived of their liberty especially against those who are escaping or attempting to escape is an extreme measure which should not be disproportionate to the legitimate objective to be achieved (to apprehend the individual) and shall always be preceded by warning appropriate to the circumstances (Art. 42 Third Geneva Convention).

The Coalition Forces detaining personnel should be provided with adequate training to deal with incidents in their internment facilities. Firearms should not be used except when a suspected offender offers armed resistance or otherwise jeopardizes the lives of others and only when less extreme measures are not sufficient to restrain or apprehend him (Article 3 of the Code of Conduct for Law Enforcement Officials and Article 9 of the Basic Principles on the Use of Force and Firearms by Law Enforcement Officials).

In every instance in which a firearm is discharged, a report should be made promptly to the competent authorities. All deaths or serious injuries of a person deprived of his liberty caused or suspected to have been caused by a sentry should be immediately followed by a proper inquiry by the Detaining Power which should ensure the prosecution of any person(s) found responsible (Art 121, Third Geneva Convention; Art. 131, Fourth Geneva Convention).

Seizure and confiscation of private belongings of persons deprived of their liberty

The International Committee of the Red Cross collected numerous allegations of seizure and confiscation of private properly (money, cars and other valuables) by the Coalition Forces in the context of arrests. In only a few cases were receipts issued to the arrested person or his family, detailing the items confiscated. This was perceived by persons deprived of their liberty as outright theft or pillage. The following examples will serve to illustrate the allegations:

[Mr A – name obscured] alleged that the Coalition Forces took US$22,000 in cash and his personal luggage during his arrest;

[Mr B – name obscured] claimed that large amounts of money and personal effects were confiscated by the Coalition Forces when he was arrested at his home on 27-28 May 2003. The items confiscated allegedly included 71,450,000 Iraqi dinars, 14,000 US dollars, two wedding rings, a video camera, a watch, real-estate property documents, his wife's residential documents, his father's will, his private diaries, as well as most of the family private documents and personal identity and other papers;

[Mr C – name obscured] claimed that his car was confiscated when he was arrested by the Coalition Forces in Basrah on 16 July 2003;

[Mr D – name obscured] claimed that Coalition Forces confiscated two million Iraqi dinars when arrested at his home on 21 August 2003;

[Mr E – name obscured] claimed that his money and two cars were confiscated when he was arrested by the Coalition Forces on 11 August 2003.

In Camp Cropper, Camp Bucco and Abu Ghraib, a system was gradually put in place whereby personal belongings in the possession of persons deprived of their liberty at the time of their arrival in these facilities which they could not keep with them (money, other valuables, spare clothing, identity papers) were registered and kept until their release. In these cases, a receipt was usually issued to the person deprived of his liberty and his belongings were returned when he was released. However, this system took no account of the property seized during arrest.

In response to property loss or damage caused to property by the Coalition Forces during raids and also to complaints regarding pension or salaries, the Coalition Forces established a compensation system open to everyone, including internees and the general public. Complaints could be filed at General Information Centers (GIC), set up under the responsibility of the Humanitarian Assistance Coordination Centers (HACC).

Supporting evidence, which is problematic given that arresting authorities rarely issue receipts, should back claims. The International Committee of the Red Cross is not yet able to assess the efficiency of this compensation system although it has had the possibility to visit one of the General Information Centers. There are nine General Information Centers in the city of Baghdad and one in the city of Mosul, there are however none in the other parts of the country therefore depriving a large number of persons of the possibility to file complaints.

In accordance with international legal provisions, the International Committee of the Red Cross reminds the authorities of the Coalition Forces that pillage is prohibited by International Humanitarian Law (Art 33, Fourth Geneva Convention), that private property may not be confiscated (Art. 46.2, 1907 Hague Convention No IV), and that an army of occupation can only take possession of cash, funds, and realizable securities which are strictly the property of the State. (Art. 53, 1907 Hague Convention No IV).

In addition, persons deprived of their liberty shall be permitted to retain articles of personal use. Valuables may not be taken from them except in accordance with an established procedure and receipts must be issued (Art. 18. 68.2, Third Geneva Convention and Art. 97, Fourth Geneva Convention).

Exposure of internees/detainees to dangerous tasks

On 3 September 2003 in Camp Bucca, three persons deprived of their liberty were severely injured by the explosion of what apparently was a cluster bomb:

[Mr F – name obscured] bilateral below-knee amputation
[Mr G – name obscured] bilateral above-knee amputation
[Mr H – name obscured] left above-knee amputation

They were part of a group of 10 persons deprived of their liberty involved in voluntary work to clear rubbish along the barbed-wire fence of the camp. They were transferred to the British Field Military Hospital where they received appropriate medical treatment. Their injuries required limb amputations.

On 23 October 2003, the International Committee of the Red Cross wrote to the officer commanding the 800th Military Police Brigade to request an investigation into the incident. The International Committee of the Red Cross encouraged the Coalition Forces not to engage persons deprived of their liberty in dangerous labour.

The International Committee of the Red Cross recommends to the authorities of the Coalition Forces that all three victims be properly compensated as provided for by both Third and Fourth Geneva Conventions (Art. 68, Third Geneva Convention and Art. 95, Fourth Geneva Convention).

Protection of persons deprived of their liberty against shelling

Since its reopening by the Coalition Forces, Abu Ghraib prison has been the target of frequent night shelling by mortars and other weapons, which resulted, on several occasions, in persons deprived of their liberty being killed or injured. During the month of July, the Commander of the facility reported at least 25 such attacks. On 16 August, three mortar rounds landed in the prison compound, killing at least five and injuring 67 persons deprived of their liberty. Subsequent attacks caused further deaths and injuries. An International Committee of the Red Cross team visited Abu Ghraib on 17 August and noticed the lack of protective measures: while the Coalition Forces personnel were living in concrete buildings, all persons deprived of their liberty were sheltered under tents in compounds which had no bunkers or any other protection, rendering them totally vulnerable to shelling.

Persons deprived of their liberty alleged that they had not been advised of what to do to protect themselves in the event of shelling. They were dismayed and felt that the authorities 'did not care'. After these attacks, security was improved around the prison compound to reduce the risk of further attacks. However, steps taken to ensure the protection of persons deprived of their liberty remained insufficient The inmates were allowed to fill and place sandbags around the perimeter of each tent. By late October, sandbags had not been placed around all tents and those sandbags that were in place did not offer adequate protection from shelling or projectile explosions.

In accordance with International Humanitarian law provisions, the International Committee of the Red Cross reminds the authorities of the Coalition

Forces that the detaining power must not set up places of internment in areas particularly exposed to the dangers of war (Art. 23.1, Third Geneva Convention and Art. 83, Fourth Geneva Convention). In all places of internment exposed to air raids and other hazards of war, shelters adequate in number and structure to ensure the necessary protection must be made available. In the event of an alarm, the internees must be free to enter such shelters as quickly as possible (Art. 23.2, Third Geneva Convention and Art 86, Fourth Geneva Convention). When a place of internment is found to be unsafe, persons deprived of their liberty should be transferred to other places of internment, offering adequate security and living conditions in accordance with the Third and Fourth Geneva Conventions.

Conclusion

This International Committee of the Red Cross report documents serious violations of International Humanitarian Law relating to the conditions of treatment of the persons deprived of their liberty held by the Coalition Forces in Iraq. In particular, it establishes that persons deprived of their liberty face the risk of being subjected to a process of physical and psychological coercion, in some cases tantamount to torture, in the early stages of the internment process.

Once the interrogation process is over, the conditions of treatment for the persons deprived of their liberty generally improve, except in the 'High Value Detainee' section at Baghdad International Airport where persons deprived of their liberty have been held for nearly 23 hours a day in strict solitary confinement in small concrete cells devoid of daylight, an internment regime which does not comply with provisions of the Third and Fourth Geneva Conventions.

During internment, persons deprived of their liberty also risk being victims of disproportionate and excessive use of force on the part of detaining authorities attempting to restore order in the event of unrest or to prevent escapes.

Another serious violation of International Humanitarian Law described in the report is the Coalition Force's inability or lack of will to set up a system of notifications of arrests for the families of persons deprived of liberty in Iraq. This violation of provisions of International Humanitarian Law causes immense distress among persons deprived of their liberty and their families, the latter fearing that their relatives unaccounted for are dead. The uncaring behavior of the Coalition Forces and their inability to quickly provide accurate information on persons deprived of their liberty for the families concerned also seriously affects the image of the Occupying Powers amongst the Iraqi population.

In addition to recommendations highlighted in the report relating to conditions of internment, information given to persons deprived of their liberty upon arrest, and the need to investigate violations of International Humanitarian Law and to prosecute those found responsible, the International Committee of the Red Cross wishes particularly to remind the Coalition Forces of their duty:

● to respect at all times the human dignity, physical integrity and cultural sensitivity of persons deprived of their liberty held under their control;

● to set up a system of notifications of arrests to ensure that the families of

persons deprived of their liberty are quickly and accurately informed;
● to prevent all forms of ill-treatment and moral or physical coercion of persons deprived of their liberty in connection with interrogations;
● to instruct the arresting and detaining authorities that causing serious bodily injury or serious harm to the health of protected persons is prohibited under the Third and Fourth Geneva Conventions;
● to set up an internment regime that ensures respect for the psychological integrity and human dignity of the persons deprived of their liberty;
● to ensure that battle group units arresting individuals and staff in charge of internment facilities receive adequate training enabling them to operate in a proper manner and fulfill their responsibilities without resorting to ill-treatment or using excessive force.

The practices described in this report are prohibited under International Humanitarian Law. They warrant serious attention by the Coalition Forces. In particular, the Coalition Forces should review their policies and practices, take corrective action and improve the treatment of prisoners of war and other protected persons under their authority. This report is part of the bilateral and confidential dialogue undertaken by the International Committee of the Red Cross with the Coalition Forces. In the future, the International Committee of the Red Cross will continue its bilateral and confidential dialogue with the Coalition Forces in accordance with provisions of International Humanitarian Law, on the basis of its monitoring of the conditions of arrest, interrogation and internment of persons deprived of their liberty held by the Coalition Forces.

KILLINGS OF CIVILIANS IN BASRA AND AL-'AMARA

With grateful acknowledgements to Amnesty International who issued this report on 11 May 2004.

More than a year after the occupation of Iraq, civilians are still being killed unlawfully every day by Coalition Forces, armed groups and individuals. In recent weeks hundreds of civilians have been killed as clashes between Coalition Forces and armed groups and individuals opposed to the occupation have intensified. In Falluja alone, at least 600 people, including many children, have been killed during clashes between Coalition Forces and insurgents.[1] On 4 April US forces launched major operations in Falluja following the killing, burning and mutilation of four US private security guards by insurgents on 31 March. Clashes have also erupted between Coalition Forces and supporters of the Shi'a leader Muqtada al-Sadr in parts of Baghdad and in several other cities and towns. These clashes were prompted by the closure at the end of March of *al-Hawza al-Natiqa* newspaper, mouthpiece of Muqtada al-Sadr's group, and the arrest of one of his closest aides, Mustafa al-Ya'qubi, on charges relating to the April 2003 assassination in al-Najaf of well-known Shi'a cleric 'Abd al-Majid al-Khoie. The newspaper was closed down by order of Ambassador Paul Bremer, head of the Coalition Provisional Authority, on the grounds that it was inciting violence.

In southern Iraq, dozens or possibly hundreds of civilians have been executed by armed groups and individuals since the start of the occupation. Killings often take place in the street in broad daylight. The violence is fuelled by the easy availability of small arms. Individuals, even the police, are reluctant to talk about these killings because they fear that speaking out will endanger their lives and those of their families. No one claims responsibility for these killings. The fact that the perpetrators are anonymous and the motivation often unclear only adds to people's sense of fear and insecurity. Iraqis appear to have no confidence that the British Army or the Iraqi police can protect them from such attacks or that the perpetrators will be held accountable before the law. It is therefore no surprise that in a recent poll conducted in Iraq by Oxford Research International, nearly 65 per cent of people interviewed said the restoration of public security in Iraq was their top priority.[2]

The United Kingdom (UK) Ministry of Defence has said that UK forces have been involved in the killing of 37 civilians since 1 May 2003. It acknowledges that this figure is not comprehensive as it is sometimes impossible for soldiers to confirm the number of casualties in a specific incident. In several cases documented by Amnesty International, UK soldiers opened fire and killed Iraqi civilians in circumstances where there was apparently no imminent threat of death or serious injury to themselves or others.

All governments are under a duty to take action to secure the right to life. In the case of suspected killings, such as those carried out by soldiers or police, a government must launch a thorough, competent, independent and impartial investigation into the allegations and bring to justice anyone reasonably suspected of responsibility. Despite this, the British Army has not even opened an investigation into many cases where civilians have been killed by UK forces in Iraq. Where investigations have been opened, the British Royal Military Police (RMP), which is responsible for conducting the investigations, has been highly secretive and has provided families with little or no information about the progress or conclusions of investigations.

Governments must also take action to prevent abuses of the right to life by individuals and armed groups. All killings must be investigated thoroughly and anyone suspected of responsibility must be put on trial. However, the Iraqi Police Service appears to be unable or unwilling to launch serious investigations into the frequent killings of middle-ranking Ba'ath Party members or killings linked to moral or religious disputes.

Southern Iraq had until recently been spared the massive attacks that have targeted Iraqi civilians in northern and central Iraq. Amnesty International delegates were present in southern Iraq conducting research for this report when nine coordinated attacks took place in Karbala and Baghdad on 1 March 2004, killing over 150 people. Amnesty International called for such attacks to be stopped immediately and for those responsible to be brought to justice.[3] Since

March 2004 the security situation in Basra and other southern cities and towns has deteriorated. For example, on 21 April, 73 people, including 17 children, were killed when several coordinated bombs exploded at three police stations in Basra and a police academy in Zubair area. Two school buses were travelling nearby when the bombs were detonated in central Basra.

This report focuses on killings of civilians in southern Iraq, whether perpetrated by state agents, individuals or armed groups, and is based on research carried out by Amnesty International delegates in southern Iraq between 9 February and 4 March 2004. Eyewitnesses and families of victims were interviewed, and sites of killings were visited. Amnesty International delegates also interviewed a large number of Iraqi police officers, including the heads of the Iraqi Police Service in Basra and in al-'Amara, capital of Maysan Province, as well as Iraqi judges and lawyers. Delegates also met Coalition Provisional Authority (CPA) officials responsible for law and order in southern Iraq.

Amnesty International requested meetings with the Commander Legal attached to UK forces stationed in Iraq and with the Royal Military Police. Both parties refused such meetings, referring Amnesty International's delegates back to the UK Ministry of Defence. The Royal Military Police told a delegate on the telephone: 'We have nothing to say to you.' Further information on the UK government's response to killings of Iraqi civilians by UK armed forces was obtained from UK parliamentary reports.

Killings by UK forces

In a number of cases UK soldiers have opened fire and killed Iraqi civilians in circumstances where there was apparently no imminent threat of death or serious injury to themselves or others. In most such cases documented by Amnesty International, soldiers resorted to lethal force even though the use of such force did not appear to be strictly necessary in order to protect life. The following cases are just some of those studied by Amnesty International.

Killings of individuals

Wa'el Rahim Jabar
On 26 May 2003 a UK paratrooper shot and killed Wa'el Rahim Jabar, aged 20, in Hay Abu Romaneh district of al-'Amara. At that time, the security situation had not been stabilized in al-'Amara and it remained common for Iraqis to carry weapons in Hay Abu Romaneh. Wa'el Rahim Jabar was among the men assigned responsibility by the local community for protecting the area. On the day of his death, he was walking along the main street with a Kalashnikov rifle slung over his right shoulder, accompanied by two friends, Majed Jasem and Mu'taz 'Ati, who were unarmed. It was 9.10pm and dark, so they did not realize that there was a UK military foot patrol, consisting of four paratroopers with no interpreter, in the area. One of the paratroopers began shooting from a distance of about six metres, firing two rounds which struck Wa'el Rahim Jabar in the chest and neck, killing him immediately. The paratrooper reportedly fired without warning.

About 10 days later, a group of paratroopers visited the home of Daoud Salman Sajet, the victim's maternal uncle, and expressed their condolences about his nephew's death. They stressed, however, that the soldier had opened fire because the victim was carrying a weapon in public even though the British Army had warned Iraqis not to do this. In June 2003, the family's lawyer gave a CPA representative a complaint about the killing, including a request for compensation. By February 2004, the family had received no response. They were also unaware that an investigation into the killing had been initiated by the Royal Military Police.

As well as completing his education, Wa'el Rahim Jabar had been working as a baker to support his mother, wife and two children.

Hassan Hameed Naser

On 9 and 10 August 2003 there were violent demonstrations by Iraqis in Basra to protest against the lack of fuel in the city. On the second day, demonstrations were concentrated in northern Basra. In Karmat 'Ali, hundreds of youths gathered near the main transport garage in the early morning and threw stones at vehicles passing on the main road and at a patrol of three UK military armoured vehicles attached to B Company of the First Battalion the King's Regiment. Soldiers opened fire. Hassan Hameed Naser, an unemployed single man, was shot dead, apparently by the UK soldiers.

Qasem Hameed Naser, the victim's brother, told Amnesty International that he and his brother left home that morning to take public transport into central Basra. As they approached the garage, they saw young men nearby throwing stones at an armoured vehicle. Qasem Hameed Naser said that he could hear shots being fired from behind them. He thought that they came from an area close to a nearby school. Three armoured vehicles were positioned at intervals on the other side of the road. He said that suddenly a soldier positioned on the third vehicle, closest to the garage, began firing randomly. One of the rounds hit Hassan Hameed Naser's body. He was taken to Tahrir Hospital but died after an operation.

A UK military spokesman commented on the events at the time: 'There are four protests in northern Basra. They have turned into some small riots. There has been an instance where some UK soldiers came under fire, and they returned aimed shots.'

Following the killing, an officer from B Company of the First Battalion the King's Regiment visited Hassan Hameed Naser's family. He reportedly expressed his sorrow for the death but pointed out that there had been shooting during the demonstration. Another meeting between the officer and the family and representatives of the family's Khalaf 'ashira (clan) took place about 10 days later when the officer offered the family 2,000,000 Iraqi dinars (US$1,405). The family refused the offer. Later, they decided to accept it but by then a new army company had been deployed in the area and the offer no longer stood.

On 1 December Qasem Hameed Naser submitted a claim for compensation to the Area Claims Office, which handles claims for compensation brought against UK forces in Iraq. The following day the Area Claims Officer rejected it because it 'revealed no evidence to substantiate... [the] claim'. An Iraqi interpreter who worked with the UK military intervened on behalf of the family and as a result the Area Claims Officer decided to reconsider the application for compensation.

Information provided by the UK Minister of State for the Armed Forces on 19 January 2004 indicated that no investigation had been launched by the UK military authorities into the killing of Hassan Hameed Naser.

Hazam Jumah Kati' and 'Abed 'Abd al-Karim Hassan

On the evening of 4 August 2003, soldiers from the B Company of the First Battalion the King's Regiment opened fire in Hay al-Shuhada, al-Majdiyeh, killing Hazam Jumah Kati', an unemployed man aged about 60, and 'Abed 'Abd al-Karim Hassan, an unemployed man aged about 25. According to both men's families, gunfire was heard in the area at about 11pm. Hazam Jumah Kati' and 'Abed 'Abd al-Karim Hassan left their houses, which are close to each other on the same street, to find out what was happening. It later emerged that Iraqis nearby had fired into the air to mark the death of a local sheikh.

It was very dark that evening as there was no electricity. Both men were reportedly unarmed. Jumah Kati', Hazam's father, also went outside to see what was happening and stood near 'Abed 'Abd al-Karim Hassan's home. About 15 minutes after the gunfire, a UK military patrol arrived and parked near where he was standing. By that stage Hazam Jumah Kati' and 'Abed 'Abd al-Karim Hassan were both walking back home along the narrow road. The patrol opened fire. Jumah Kati' told Amnesty International: 'Then a man came and told me: "There are people dead on the road. They killed two people". A group of us went to the patrol. One of us spoke English a bit. He asked: "Whom did you kill?" The soldier told him to accompany him [to the bodies]. I said to Captain Tai: "Why did you kill?" He said: "I am sorry. There was a mistake. I apologize." I repeated the question: "Why did you kill them?" He said: "It was dark. One colleague was in a hurry. I am sorry. I don't accept such behaviour."'

Hazam Jumah Kati' was hit by seven bullets in his chest and stomach. He died immediately. 'Abed 'Abd al-Karim Hassan was hit by five bullets in the right arm, the right leg, the chest and lower body and died later from his injuries.

Lieutenant Colonel Ciaran Griffin, Commander of the First Battalion the King's Regiment, accompanied by a group of officers, went to Hay al-Shuhada' on about 20 August to meet representatives of the families' 'ashira, the Beni Skein. He apologized for the deaths but made it clear that the army was not prepared to give compensation because it did not accept responsibility for the deaths. Instead he offered to make a 'donation' to both families.

The British Army sent a letter to the Beni Skein 'ashira on 17 August 2003 signed by Lieutenant Colonel Ciaran Griffin. It states:

> On the night of 4 August 2003 a patrol from the 1st Battalion The King's Regiment observed a lot of shooting from the area of Al Majdiyah and believed that there was a dangerous gun battle taking place. They drove to the edge of the village and went in on foot to investigate. The night was very dark, as there was no electricity for street

lighting and the moon had set. The patrol encountered two men, who appeared to be armed and a direct threat to their lives, so they opened fire and killed them.

In retrospect it became clear that the heavy shooting in Al Majdiyah was in sympathy for the funeral of a local man and that the two men who were shot by the British patrol had not intended to attack anyone. We greatly regret the deaths of Hasim Jumah Gattah and Abed Abdul-Kareem Hassan and we hope to work with the Ben Skein and all other tribes to avoid this type of misunderstanding in the future.

Although all good people are allowed to keep 2 weapons at home and another at their place of work, weapons are forbidden on the streets to avoid these misunderstandings with the Army and Police. If these rules had been obeyed this tragic event would not have happened.

Although the British Government cannot agree to pay compensation for these deaths, I have made a small donation to help their families through this sad period. This donation of 2,000,000 Iraqi Dinars for the family of Abed Abdu-Kareem Hassan and 3,000,000 Iraqi Dinars for the family of Hasim Jumah Gattah, should not preclude any future Iraqi government from paying compensation, if this becomes their policy.

Information provided by the UK Minister of State for the Armed Forces on 19 January 2004 indicates that no investigation was initiated by the UK military authorities into these killings.

Hanan Saleh Matrud

On 21 August 2003 a soldier from B Company of the First Battalion the King's Regiment shot and killed Hanan Saleh Matrud, an eight-year-old girl, in Karmat 'Ali. There are distinct differences in the accounts of what happened between Iraqi witnesses and the victim's family on one hand and the First Battalion the King's Regiment on the other. The latter's position is set out in a letter provided to the family and dated 12 October 2003. The letter states:

> 21AUG03. A patrol of two Warrior vehicles of B Company 1 KINGS was on task travelling on the western track of Qarmat Ali. The area of Qarmat Ali was at this time known to be hostile towards Coalition Forces. As the patrol moved north along the track it was engaged by heavy stone throwing from a number of mobs. A soldier concerned for his own safety and the safety of his patrol fired a warning shot into the air in an attempt to disperse the stone throwers. This had the desired effect, with the mob taking flight.
>
> A number of minutes had passed with the patrol assessing the situation and calming the local people. The patrol then noticed a crowd of people running towards them from an area of buildings with a girl who had been cut across the abdominal area. The eight year old girl was Hanan Salih Matrood. She remained conscious but was obviously distressed and it was evident that the wound was serious. After being transferred to the Czech Hospital in Northern Basrah, Hanan died on the morning of 22AUG03.
>
> The suggestion was that this wound sustained as a result of the warning shot, which has not been proven, but accepted as a possibility.

The letter, which was given to the family in English, also stated that Saleh Matrud, Hanan's father, agreed with the letter. However, Hanan's family denies that there was any stonethrowing when the soldier opened fire. One eyewitness,

Mizher Jabbar Yassin, said that an armoured vehicle stopped near the entrance to the alley which leads to Hanan's home, and three or four soldiers got out. A group of children, including Hanan, gathered about 60 or 70 metres from the vehicle inside the alley, attracted by the soldiers. Hanan was standing in the alley about 60 to 70 metres from the armoured vehicle. Suddenly a soldier aimed and fired a shot which hit Hanan in her lower torso. Hanan's uncle, Fellah Matrud, carried her to the armoured vehicle. At first the soldiers did not want to take her to hospital, but later did. She died the following day after an operation.

Shortly after Hanan's death, an officer from B Company, 'Major Gary', stationed at the nearby al-Hartha checkpoint, visited the family and proposed a truce between their 'ashira, the Qatrani, and the British Army. The family and the 'ashira refused a truce without compensation. In October, Saleh Matrud went to al-Hartha checkpoint to follow up on the question of compensation. An officer from B Company told him that a future Iraqi government would decide whether to compensate him and for this reason the company provided him with the letter of 12 October. This information was clearly inaccurate as a procedure for submitting claims for compensation for personal injury through the Area Claims Office at the airport had already been established.

According to Hanan's family, the military police photographed the area and interviewed witnesses the day after the killing, and photographed Hanan's body in the hospital. However, information provided by the UK Minister of State for the Armed Forces on 19 January 2004 indicates that no investigation was initiated by the UK military authorities into this killing.

Walid Fayay Mazban

Walid Fayay Mazban, a 42-year-old driver, was shot dead on 24 August 2003 at a temporary checkpoint in Sikek, Basra, by a soldier from the First Battalion the King's Regiment. He was the sole breadwinner for his wife, two children and two parents.

On the evening of 24 August UK soldiers were staffing a temporary checkpoint at the Suq al-Hattin crossroads on the edge of Sikek. According to an eyewitness, three soldiers stood across the northern side of the road, one was on the southwestern side and another was on the northeastern side. The area was very dark because there was no electricity. Saddam Hussein Danan, a neighbour of Walid Fayay Mazban who witnessed the killing, said:

> I was on a bicycle about 50 meters behind Walid's vehicle. It was about 8.30pm. He was driving normally and suddenly there was gunfire. It was dark. There was no light. I did not hear anything before the gunfire. There were maybe six or seven shots. When I heard the gunfire I ran away.

Walid Fayay Mazban was fired on from behind after he had turned his minibus left at the junction. According to his family, he was apparently fired on by a soldier who was standing on the southwestern side of the crossroads. Walid Fayay Mazban sustained multiple bullet injuries in his lower back, according to medical reports. His family reported that there were three bullet holes in the back of the minibus, which remains impounded by the UK military. Following the shooting, Walid Fayay Mazban was transported by military ambulance to Fayha Hospital, where he died the following day.

Kadhem Finjan Hussein, formerly Chairman of the Local Councils in North Basra, who participated in negotiations between Walid Fayay Mazban's family and the British Army, told Amnesty International that the representatives from the British Army had told him that soldiers at the checkpoint had seen Walid Fayay Mazban's vehicle swerving in a suspicious manner. They had shouted 'stop' in English at the vehicle. After it failed to stop, it had been fired upon. Walid Fayay Mazban did not understand English and it is possible that he did not even hear the order to stop. Nothing suspicious was found by the British Army when the vehicle was searched.

Later in August, an officer from the King's Regiment attended a meeting with representatives of the family's 'ashira, al-Bubsayri, the family and Hussein Kadhem Finjan Hussein. According to Hussein Kadhem Finjan Hussein, the UK officer offered to pay 2,000,000 Iraqi dinars ($US1,405) to assist the family. The officer stressed that this did not amount to admission of any legal liability for the killing. After initial refusal, the family accepted the sum. The family has not been told of any investigation into the circumstances of Walid Fayay Mazban's death. However, on 19 January 2004, the UK Minister of State for the Armed Forces stated that an investigation had been launched into the killing.

As'ad Kadhem Jasem

On 4 September 2003 at least one soldier from the First Battalion the King's Regiment shot dead As'ad Kadhem Jasem, a taxi driver who was married with one son, at al-Hartha checkpoint, north of Basra.

As'ad Kadhem Jasem had approached al-Hartha checkpoint at speed in his taxi at around 11pm. Haidar Hisham Jasem, who was sitting next to him, told Amnesty International that As'ad Kadhem Jasem was driving at speed because he was worried that he might be stopped by thieves trying to steal his taxi. There was no electricity in the area, so everything was dark, and they failed to see the barrier blocking part of the lane as they approached the checkpoint. As'ad Kadhem Jasem swerved and managed to stop at the second barrier, which was by a building where UK troops were based. After the car stopped soldiers opened fire from the watchtower located behind the car near the first barrier. Two bullets penetrated the taxi and As'ad Kadhem Jasem was killed by one that hit him in the back of the head.

Haidar Hisham Jasem was held for questioning at the checkpoint. He only discovered later from UK soldiers that As'ad Kadhem Jasem had been killed. No one from the UK military has contacted him in connection with an investigation. He says that he was told by an officer through an interpreter that the soldiers involved would be put on trial.

'Ammar Kadhem Jasem, the brother of As'ad Kadhem Jasem, told Amnesty International that no one from the British Army contacted the family after the death. In October, he went to al-Hartha checkpoint and provided information about the killing and a request for compensation to an officer at the checkpoint. At the end of 2003, members of the family went to the Presidential Palace, where the CPA and Brigade Headquarters are located, to follow up on the claim, but got no response. On 22 February 2004, 'Ammar Kadhem Jasem contacted the Area Claims Office by telephone to inquire about lodging a compensation claim. He was discouraged because an Iraqi interpreter told him that he was required to submit the name and unit of the soldier who had killed his brother. An Amnesty International delegate called later that day to clarify the situation. The Area Claims Officer stated that the information had been incorrect and explained that claimants were required to go to Basra International Airport and complete an application form.

Information provided by the UK Minister of State for the Armed Forces on 19 January 2004 indicates that no investigation was initiated by the UK military authorities into this killing.

Hilal Finjan Salman

Hilal Finjan Salman, a father of nine, had worked for 35 years as a guard for al-Ma'qal Girls Junior High School, located across the road from Ma'qal port. He was licensed to carry a weapon, a 10-bore Seminov rifle, to protect the school. He was also required to wear a luminous orange jacket when he carried his gun to show that he was authorized to carry a weapon. However, neither the British Army nor the Iraqi authorities had issued him with such a jacket.

Early in the morning of 4 October 2003 thousands of former Iraqi soldiers started to gather near the port to try to collect their salaries. UK soldiers were deployed inside the port and on its perimeter wall, including the area facing the school. Rioting broke out from early morning and people started to throw stones at the soldiers. From about 9.15am, demonstrators started to force themselves into the school compound. Hundreds of men entered the compound. The school employees, concerned about the safety of the more than 200 girls attending the school, took the girls into the school hall. According to some present in the school, Hilal Finjan Salman fired twice into the air from one of the schoolyards to intimidate the men. He then went up onto the roof facing the port and started to patrol from there, holding his rifle in one hand. All witnesses interviewed by Amnesty International agree that he did not open fire from the roof. At about 10.15am a UK soldier, standing above the port wall, fired on Hilal Finjan Salman, hitting his right shoulder and chest, killing him. UK soldiers entered the school and took Hilal Finjan Salman's body to hospital.

On 8 November Hassan Hilal Finjan Salman, the victim's son, submitted a claim for compensation. On 12 November the Area Claims Officer responded in writing saying that he would contact the family when he had completed his investigation. The family had received no further information on the progress of their application by February 2004. No investigation has apparently been initiated by the UK military authorities into the death. On 6 January 2004, the UK Minister of State for the Armed Forces said: 'On 4 October, on the periphery of a demonstration, UK soldiers killed an Iraqi gunman in self-defence. His automatic weapon and ammunition were recovered.'

Ghanem Kadhem Kati'
Following the overthrow of the Iraqi government, Ghanem Kadhem Kati', 22, returned home to Basra from exile in Iran. He started working with his father as a moneychanger. On the afternoon of 1 January 2004, a wedding celebration took place in Beit Asfar near his home during which bullets were fired in the air to celebrate the marriage. About 15 minutes later, two members of the UK armed forces took up positions by a low wall opposite the house of Ghanem Kadhem Kati'. They were apparently members of a boat patrol which operates on the Shatt al-Arab Waterway. A neighbour reported seeing one of the soldiers crouching at the end of the wall and aiming his rifle towards Ghanem Kadhem Kati'. The neighbour reportedly tried to warn the soldiers not to fire and to explain that the earlier shooting had been related to a wedding. After about seven or eight minutes, the soldier fired at Ghanem Kadhem Kati' from a distance of about 50 metres. Ghanem Kadhem Kati' was unarmed and standing with his back to the soldiers near the door of his home. Two bullets went through his body, killing him. Another bullet grazed the edge of the house and two others went through the door.

The Royal Military Police apparently launched an investigation into the killing. In mid-January, five eyewitnesses were interviewed by the Royal Military Police and later that month soldiers photographed the house and surrounding area. In February, the body of Ghanem Kadhem Kati' was exhumed and flown to Basra by helicopter for examination at a military hospital. Soldiers also removed the front door of the house, which contained two bullet holes. The Royal Military Police distributed a leaflet in English and Arabic asking witnesses to come forward and testify. DNA samples were taken from close relatives. No one, however, advised the family of Ghanem Kadhem Kati' of the procedures for applying to the Area Claims Officer for compensation.

Killings of demonstrators

On 10 January 2004, at least three Iraqis, **Muhannad Jasem Jureid**, 23, **Rahim Hanoun 'Adiou**, 35, and **Maher 'Abd al-Wahid Muften**, 17, were killed during an unauthorized demonstration in al-'Amara. At least 11 others were injured.

In the early morning hundreds of Iraqis started to gather near the Governorate building on Dijleh Street, hoping to register their names for new jobs in the Iraqi Civil Defence Corps. It then became apparent that no jobs were available. A protest began and turned violent. Many demonstrators threw stones at the Iraqi police, and some threw explosive devices. The police and the British Army, as well as some eyewitnesses interviewed by Amnesty International delegates, said that there was also shooting from the crowd. Some of the demonstrators broke into the Governorate building and stole things. Some others burgled nearby shops.

At some time after 9am more than 100 members of the Emergency Brigade, which is part of the Iraqi Police Service, were deployed. This new force had been set up in mid-2003. Most if not all of its members had had no policing experience prior to their recruitment. They also had received no training in riot control and were equipped only with Kalashnikov rifles. Its members were almost exclusively drawn from the Muhammadiya 'ashira and are perceived as being closely allied to the Governor of Maysan Province, who is from the same 'ashira.

The Emergency Brigade began to fire randomly while advancing towards the Governorate building and the demonstrators. After a short time, UK soldiers from the First Battalion of the Light Infantry were deployed and placed themselves between the Emergency Force and the crowd. Muhannad Jasem Jureid and Maher 'Abd al-Wahid Muften were killed between 10am and 11am in Baghdad Street. Rahim Hanoun 'Adiou was shot and killed at about 3pm in Dijleh Street, outside the Rafidin Bank, reportedly by UK soldiers.

On 26 February Amnesty International discussed the incident with the Chief of Police of Maysan Province. He stated that the Iraqi police 'may have opened fire' but was not prepared to confirm that this had happened. He did not admit that the police had been responsible for killing or injuring any of the demonstrators. A British Army spokesman stated at the time of the demonstration that 'one, maybe two [of the dead] were possibly killed by UK troops... Those troops were firing in self-defence. It was quite clear that a number of objects were thrown at the UK troops, possibly grenades. I can assure everybody that they only fired in self-defence.' On 26 January the Minister of State for the Armed Forces stated that UK forces shot two Iraqis, one of whom subsequently died. He continued: 'Both were preparing to throw grenades, having already thrown other grenades or explosive devices at UK vehicles, and were a threat to our forces and to local Iraqi civilians.'

At the time, the media reported that five or six Iraqis had been killed. However, only three bodies were transferred to the Office of Forensic Medicine at al-Sadr General Hospital. A doctor at the hospital said that a family removed from the hospital the body of another person, who had been shot and injured in the demonstration and later died, before the body could be transferred to the Office of Forensic Medicine.

Maher 'Abd al-Wahid Muften and Rahim Hanoun 'Adiou both died of a single bullet wound in the back of the head. Muhannad Jasem Jureid died of a bullet wound to his body. The head of the Office of Forensic Medicine told Amnesty International delegates that no autopsies were carried out because the cause of death was obvious. He said there were no bullets left in the bodies but that, in any event, the office in al-'Amara would not have had the capacity to identify the type of ammunition used.

The Felonies Court of al-'Amara, responding to a request from the Public Safety Committee, the public body responsible for overseeing the work of the police in Maysan Province, opened an investigation into the events of 10 January. According to the three judges who are members of the investigation committee, the purpose of the investigation is to collect evidence and to bring charges against criminal suspects, who will be tried by the Felonies Court.

The committee is facing several difficulties. One is the absence of ballistic evidence and autopsy reports. The legal investigators, who are working under the supervision of the committee, were unable to inspect and gather material evidence, including spent rounds, from the area where the demonstration took place. Another difficulty is the reluctance of witnesses to come forward. The Coordinator of the Coalition Provisional Authority and the Commanding Officer of the Coalition Forces in Maysan Province wrote jointly to the head of the Court of Appeal in Maysan Province welcoming the creation of the investigation committee, urging everyone to cooperate with it and offering to provide assistance to the committee. As of 28 February, the committee had not requested any assistance from the Coalition Provisional Authority or the Coalition Forces. The court would be unable to compel any members of the UK forces to testify before it because they are not subject to the jurisdiction of the Iraqi courts.

Investigations

United Kingdom and other international military forces in Iraq enjoy immunity from Iraqi criminal and civil law; they are subject to the exclusive jurisdiction of their own states.[4] It is therefore crucial that the procedures established for investigating and prosecuting suspected unlawful killings of Iraqi civilians by UK forces are adequate and conform with international human rights standards, including Article 22 of the Basic Principles (see 'International standards' below). These procedures are the only means by which UK forces can be held accountable for their actions.

In a series of statements in the United Kingdom parliament, defence ministers have outlined the circumstances in which investigations are conducted into the killings of Iraqi civilians. A minister stated on 7 January 2004: 'The local commander reviews the circumstances to determine whether the UK forces involved acted within their rules of engagement. If he judges that they did – for example, they were returning fire against the deceased, having first been fired at themselves – no further action is taken other than a report of the incident being prepared and retained. If there is any doubt for whatever reason about the circumstances, the commanding officer must initiate an investigation by the Royal Military Police.'

According to the United Kingdom Minister of State for the Armed Forces, as of 2 February 2004, 37 deaths of civilians involving UK troops had been recorded since 1 May 2003. Of these, only 18 had been investigated by the Special Investigations Branch (SIB) of the Royal Military Police.

UK defence ministers' statements in parliament indicate that as of 19 January 2004, the Royal Military Police had conducted investigations into five cases where civilians were allegedly killed as a result of being shot by UK forces: 'Ali Salim 'Aziz, Jabar Wa'el Rahim, Walid Fayay Mazban, Hassan Sabah Latif al-Batat and Athir Karim Khalif. In three of these cases it was found that troops had behaved in accordance with their rules of engagement and that there was no case to answer. In the case of Athir Karim Khalif, the investigation was ongoing. One case had been referred to the Army Prosecuting Authority to determine whether charges would be brought. It appeared from Amnesty International's research that the Special Investigations Branch was also investigating the killing of Ghanem Kadhem Kati', although ministers have not mentioned this case.

After the Royal Military Police conducts an investigation, a report is submitted, together with supporting evidence, to the appropriate commanding officer and to the Army Legal Services. The Army Legal Services then advises the commanding officer whether there is a prima-facie case for disciplinary action. In serious cases, the Army Legal Services will advise the commanding officer on the procedure for referral to a higher authority and, if appropriate, on to the Army Prosecuting Authority. As of 19 January 2004, one case of a civilian killing had been referred to the Army Prosecuting Authority to determine whether charges would be brought.

Amnesty International is concerned that the decision to refer cases of civilian killings for investigation lies exclusively with commanding officers, who clearly lack the requisite level of independence and impartiality to conclude whether UK forces acted within their rules of engagement. Amnesty International has identified cases, set out above, of civilian killings where UK forces may have opened fire in breach of international standards on the use of force and no investigation has been conducted, presumably because commanding officers did not regard it as necessary to refer these incidents to the Royal Military Police.

Royal Military Police investigations are shrouded in secrecy and lack the level of public scrutiny required by international standards. In response to a question by a UK member of parliament requesting the names of the regiments that had been responsible for the detention of six Iraqis who had died in custody, the Minister of State for the Armed Forces responded on 8 March 2004: 'We do not release details of units who are involved in any incident that has been the subject of an Special Investigations Branch investigation, unless the case is referred for court martial.' Reports of Special Investigations Branch investigations are not published although the Minister of State for the Armed Forces has said that 'while the findings of investigations are subject to legal, operational and other security constraints, there may be some circumstances in which we are able to release certain details to entitled persons.'

Amnesty International met the families of 'Ali Salim 'Aziz, Jabar Wa'el Rahim, Walid Fayay Mazban, Hassan Sabah Latif al-Batat, Athir Karim Khalif and Ghanem Kadhem Kati', who had all apparently been killed by UK forces in Iraq. Royal Military Police investigations into these cases had either been completed or were ongoing. In general these families had not been given any information by the British Army, even verbally, about the progress or conclusions of Royal Military Police investigations. The Royal Military Police's contact with the families appeared to be confined to evidence-gathering. Three families appeared to be unaware that an investigation had been opened – Amnesty International learned about these investigations from parliamentary reports.

Amnesty International does not believe that the Royal Military Police is the appropriate body to conduct investigations into killings of civilians by UK soldiers because of its unsatisfactory record regarding these investigations.

In the case of the al-'Amara demonstration killings on 10 January, Amnesty International believes that the criminal investigation being conducted by the Felonies Court is not sufficiently wide-ranging and transparent to comply with international standards on investigations of suspected unlawful killing. These standards require that the investigation determines the cause, manner and time of death, the person responsible, and any pattern or practice that may have brought about the death. According to the investigating committee's members, such a committee does not normally make its findings public because its focus is to identify criminal suspects who should be charged and brought to trial.

Reparation

According to Coalition Provisional Authority Order 17, the United Kingdom is responsible for handling claims for personal injury and death attributed to its forces in a manner consistent with UK law. In a letter sent to Amnesty International on 3 March 2004, the Senior Policy Adviser of the Headquarters Multi National Division (South East) Operation Telic set out the procedures for claims for compensation against UK military forces in Iraq. For a claim to be upheld, the applicant must demonstrate on the balance of probabilities that damage or loss is the result of an act of negligence by a member of the UK forces when acting in his/her official duties. Claims for loss or damage occurring prior to the cessation of decisive combat activities on 1 May 2003 are not acceptable on the basis that there is no legal liability to compensate for loss or damage sustained during hostilities.

In Iraq the responsibility for dealing with all such claims against UK forces is vested in the Area Claims Officer. A claimant must submit a claim in writing to the Area Claims Officer, stating all the relevant facts and enclosing appropriate evidence. This is normally done by the individual going to the main gate of Basra International Airport where the Area Claims Officer registers the claim. The Area Claims Officer then investigates the allegations with the appropriate unit and upon completion of that investigation the claimant is notified of the decision on their claim. If their claim is successful the claimant is 'reasonably compensated based on local levels of quantum', derived from Iraqi civil law levels that have been provided by a judge in Basra. According to the UK Minister of State for the Armed Forces, Iraqi civilians who receive compensation payments are required to sign a declaration accepting the offer and stating that they understand it to be 'a full and final settlement of all claims whatsoever relating to the incident'.

Where a claim against UK troops arises from activity that would not give rise to a legal liability to pay compensation under English law, an *ex gratia* payment may be made to the injured person or to the family of the deceased where this would be in accordance with local custom or directed to meet a particular urgent humanitarian need.

The Minister of State for the Armed Forces stated on 5 January 2004 that 23 compensation claims for compensation for deaths allegedly caused by UK forces since 1 May 2003 had been submitted.[5] Of these, seven had been repudiated, 13 were still under investigation, and three had received compensation payment, amounting in total to £8,125.

As we have seen, in practice many families whose relatives have been killed by UK forces are not advised, when they come into contact with UK forces, of the procedures for applying for compensation. In several cases, UK forces have even provided families with wrong information, suggesting that they can only apply for compensation from a future Iraqi government or determining themselves that compensation is not payable.

Basra International Airport, where the Area Claims Officer is located, is not easily accessible to Iraqis, even those living in Basra. Public transport to this relatively remote area is prohibitively expensive for a poor family. Applicants must wait at the main gate to the airport, where there is no shelter from the sun, while soldiers try to contact the Area Claims Officer. Many complain that the Area Claims Officer is often not available to speak to them. They also complain that there are long delays in processing their applications. Families have very little idea of the criteria and procedures for consideration of their applications for compensation and are not provided with any written explanatory information. They do not have the opportunity to review and respond to information provided to the Area Claims Officer by the unit involved in the incident. If their claim is rejected, they receive what appears to be a standard response from the Area Claims Officer which does not provide detailed reasons for the rejection of their application. Most of the families interviewed by Amnesty International who had actually managed to submit applications to the Area Compensation Officer had little or no confidence in the process because of the lack of information and the delays. However, most of these families had made considerable efforts to follow up on their applications because of their bad economic situation.

Most families are not represented by lawyers. Many Iraqi lawyers in Basra and al-'Amara expressed to Amnesty International their lack of confidence in the compensation system, which they perceive as bureaucratic, slow and unfair to the applicant.

Some families have received *ex gratia* payments from UK forces. In most cases these payments have been negotiated between the British Army and representatives of an 'ashira. The payments are very small and are normally represented as being a contribution to assist the family. However, other families of civilians killed by the British Army have received nothing, even though they were also suffering economic hardship. The impression gained by Amnesty International is that such *ex gratia* payments have often been made to 'buy off' particular tribal or political interests which could make problems for the British Army. Negotiations with representatives of an 'ashira, structures which are patriarchal and represent the interests of a broad group of families, may not be the best way to ensure that such contributions reach the victims' immediate families, particularly dependent female relatives and children.

International standards

The United Kingdom recognizes that it is an occupying power in Iraq and therefore the conduct of its armed forces is regulated by international humanitarian law, including the Fourth Geneva Convention relative to the

Protection of Civilian Persons in Time of War (Fourth Geneva Convention) and the Protocol Additional to the Geneva Conventions of 12 August 1949, and relating to the Protection of Victims of International Armed Conflicts (Protocol I).[6] Article 27 of the Fourth Geneva Convention emphasizes that people protected by the Convention 'are entitled, in all circumstances, to respect for their persons, their honour, their family rights, their religious convictions and practices, and their manners and customs.' It also requires the occupying power to treat protected persons humanely and provide them with protection, particularly from threats and acts of violence. Article 51 of Protocol 1 states that civilians should never be the object of attack.

The United Kingdom is obliged to apply in Iraq the provisions of the human rights treaties which it has ratified, as well as those which Iraq has ratified. In a situation of belligerent occupation, international human rights law complements and reinforces provisions of international humanitarian law, by providing content and standards of interpretation, for example on the use of force and firearms in non-combat situations.

Both the United Kingdom and Iraq are parties to the International Covenant on Civil and Political Rights.[7] The United Kingdom has also ratified the European Convention for the Protection of Human Rights and Fundamental Freedoms which is also applicable to the conduct of its armed forces in Iraq.[8] Article 6 of the International Covenant and Article 2 of the European Convention guarantee the right to life. Article 4 of the International Covenant emphasizes that there can be no derogation from this right, even in time of public emergency. Article 15 of the European Convention contains a similar provision, stating that there can be no derogation from the right to life, 'except in respect of deaths resulting from lawful acts of war.'

The Iraqi Police Service, as well as the Iraqi Ministry of the Interior and the Iraqi Governing Council to which the police are formally accountable, are required to ensure the right to life, as guaranteed by the International Covenant. The police must comply with international standards on the use of force and firearms, as set out below.

Use of force and firearms by law enforcement officials

UK forces in southern Iraq are dealing with a complex situation. Sometimes they are engaged in combat activities, where the rules of international humanitarian law on the conduct of hostilities apply. At other times they find themselves dealing with law enforcement situations, for example the dispersal of violent demonstrations. In these non-combat situations, policing methods are required, in line with human rights standards of law enforcement such as the UN Code of Conduct for Law Enforcement Officials and the UN Basic Principles on the Use of Force and Firearms by Law Enforcement Officials (the Basic Principles).

The Basic Principles emphasize that the use of force, and, in particular, the use of firearms, by law enforcement officials, including soldiers, should be exceptional. Principle 9 states:

Law enforcement officials shall not use firearms against persons except in self-defence or defence of others against the imminent threat of death or serious injury, to prevent the perpetration of a particularly serious crime involving grave threat to life, to arrest a person presenting such a danger and resisting their authority, or to prevent his or her escape, and only when less extreme means are insufficient to achieve these objectives.

Principle 9 also emphasizes that 'intentional lethal use of firearms may only be made when strictly unavoidable in order to protect life.' Principle 10 requires law enforcement officials, before using firearms, to identify themselves and give a clear warning of their intent to use firearms before opening fire, 'unless to do so would unduly place the law enforcement officials at risk or would create a risk of death or serious harm to other persons.'

The Basic Principles recognize that governments must provide adequate resources to law enforcement officials to enable them to comply with these standards. Principle 2 requires governments to provide and develop equipment to allow for differentiated use of force and firearms, and to provide law enforcement officials with self-defensive equipment such as shields, helmets, bulletproof vests and bulletproof means of transportation, in order to decrease the need to use weapons of any kind.

The Rules of Engagement for Operation *Telic*, which regulate the circumstances in which UK soldiers can use force in southern Iraq, are kept secret. The UK government maintains that the rules are consistent with the Code of Conduct and Basic Principles.

Conduct of investigations of suspected unlawful killings

According to Article 22 and 23 of the Basic Principles, governments must establish effective reporting procedures for cases where law enforcement officials kill individuals, and reports must be submitted to the relevant administrative and judicial authorities. Governments must also initiate thorough, prompt and impartial investigations into these killings.

The European Court of Human Rights has developed detailed guidelines as to what a state must do in order to secure the right to life.[9] These include that an effective official investigation should be held when a person has been killed as a result of the use of force. In order for an investigation to be effective, it must be prompt, thorough, independent and impartial, and seen to be so.

The Court has ruled that the need to secure the independence of the investigation requires not only a lack of hierarchical or institutional connection on the part of the body carrying out the investigation, but also a practical independence. The investigation must also be effective in the sense that it is capable of leading to a determination of whether the force used was justified in the circumstances and, if it was not, to the identification and punishment of those responsible. The authorities must have taken reasonable steps to secure evidence relevant to the killing.

The Court has stressed that there must be a sufficient element of public scrutiny of the progress of the investigation, including decisions by the prosecuting authorities not to bring criminal charges. In all cases the victim's family must be able to be involved in the procedure to the extent necessary to safeguard their legitimate interests.

The UN Principles on the Effective Prevention and Investigation of Extra-Legal, Arbitrary and Summary Executions set out authoritative guidelines on how the United Kingdom should seek to secure the right to life in responding to suspected cases of such unlawful killings. Principle 9 requires 'thorough, prompt and impartial investigations of all suspected cases of extra-legal, arbitrary and summary executions, including eases where complaints by relatives or other reliable reports suggest unnatural death in the above circumstances. Governments shall maintain investigative offices and procedures to undertake such inquiries. The purpose of the investigation shall be to determine the cause, manner and time of death, the person responsible, and any pattern or practice which may have brought about that death. It shall include an adequate autopsy, collection and analysis of all physical and documentary evidence and statements from witnesses. The investigation shall distinguish between natural death, accidental death, suicide and homicide.'

Principle 12 states that, 'Families of the deceased and their legal representatives shall be informed of, and have access to, any hearing as well as all information relevant to the investigation and shall be entitled to present other evidence.'

Principle 11 indicates that governments should pursue investigations through an independent investigative commission 'in cases in which the established investigative procedures are inadequate because of lack of expertise or impartiality, because of the importance of the matter or because of the apparent existence of a pattern of abuse, and in cases where there are complaints from the family of the victim about these inadequacies or other substantial reasons.'

Killings by individuals and armed groups

Since the start of the occupation scores, possibly hundreds, of people have been deliberately killed by individuals or armed groups in southern Iraq for political reasons, including for perceived moral infractions such as selling or buying alcohol. These killings have occurred at a time when violent crime has increased dramatically. Small arms have become widespread in southern Iraq, helping to perpetuate and intensify violence. Light weapons, such as Rocket Propelled Grenades, are also easily available. Individuals are entitled to keep two small arms in their homes and one in their place of business without a licence. Firing into the air to mark weddings, funerals and or other events is common.

Dozens of political groups are operating in Basra. Members of these groups are frequently armed and some groups, particularly certain Shi'a Islamist groups, are feared by Basra's residents. In conducting research on killings related to politics or perceived moral infractions in Basra, Amnesty International met a wall of near total silence. Many people simply refused to talk about such killings. Others only spoke on condition of anonymity because they were afraid of retaliation by armed Shi'a Islamist groups.

No armed group has claimed responsibility for such killings, but there are strong indications that armed Shi'a Islamist groups are involved in at least some of them. Armed groups are clearly involved in other human rights abuses, such as kidnapping, detention and torture. Certain killings have followed similar patterns and some have involved a high degree of organization. However, some of the assassinations of former Ba'ath Party members were undoubtedly committed by individuals acting out of revenge.

Basra and Maysan provinces have been spared the massive attacks that have been directed at Iraqi civilians in northern and central Iraq. However on 18 March 2004 an improvised explosive device, weighing between 200 to 300 pounds and packed into a Mercedes car, detonated in central Basra, killing three Iraqi civilians. A UK military patrol had just passed through the area.

Killings of Ba'ath Party members and former government officials

Interviews with the Iraqi police indicate that dozens of middle-ranking Ba'ath Party members, as well as former government officials, have been killed in Basra in the past year. Iraqi police reported picking up more than 60 bodies, most of them former Ba'athists, from the streets. Most if not all had been shot in the head. The true number of bodies recovered by the police is probably much higher as officers in many police stations have been reluctant to discuss these killings with Amnesty International delegates.

On 29 August 2003, armed men kidnapped **Jawad Ja'far Naser** from his vegetable shop in al-Jaza'er Street, Basra. His body was later found in the Casino Lebanon area of Basra, a site where more than 20 bodies, most of them blindfolded, have been dumped over the past year, according to police. In one of his pockets was a note written in red ink, stating 'Jawad Ja'far Nas[er], Abu'l Khasib... party comrade and fida'i S[addam]. He participated in executions with 'Ali Hassan al-M[ajid] in Abu'l Hasib in [19]91.'

Muhsen 'Abd al-Wahid al-Hajani, a teacher in his early fifties and married with four children, held the rank of 'udu firqa in the Ba'ath Party. He lost his job as the school principal of Sayf Sa'ad School in Karmat 'Ali, Basra, as a result of the De-Baathification Order – Order No. 1 issued by the Coalition Provisional Authority on 16 May 2003 which removed senior Ba'ath Party officials holding the rank of 'udu firqa and above from employment in the state sector. On 26 October, Muhsen 'Abd al-Wahid al-Hajani left his home in Hay al-Salam, telling his family that he planned to register at the Directorate of Education in response to an announcement by the Directorate inviting teachers, who had been dismissed from their positions because of Order No. 1, to reapply for their positions or for a retirement pension. Shortly after he left the Directorate of Education, a car containing two people stopped near him. A man got out and shot him dead with a pistol. In the weeks following the announcement, at least seven dismissed teachers were killed in the same manner – all were shot dead shortly after leaving the Directorate of Education where they had registered their personal details, including the rank which they had held in the Ba'ath Party.

On the morning of 17 November 2003 **Samira Fadagh Mawhan**, a former school principal who held the rank of 'udu firqa (group member) in the Ba'ath Party, was shot dead about 50 metres from her home in a quiet residential street in Hay al-Rafidin. According to witnesses, two men, armed with a Kalashnikov rifle and a pistol, drove into the street. The man with the pistol fired at Samira Fadagh Mawhan. A witness heard the gunman say, before he opened fire: 'Ah, Samira, how many innocent people did you kill?'

Muhammad 'Aisa, 26, became an English teacher in a Basra secondary school in 2000.[10] According to his family, he had to join the Ba'ath Party in order to work in the teaching profession. On the morning of 31 December 2003, Muhammad 'Aisa dropped his wife, who is also a teacher, at her school. He then drove towards Basra University to drop off his sister and another young woman. As he was driving through al-Tuweisah area, a white Land Cruiser with two men in it drove in front of his car and blocked the road. One of the men got out and fired five bullets into Muhammad 'Aisa's chest with a pistol, killing him instantly. The family does not know who killed him or why. One possibility is that he was killed because he was a Ba'ath Party member.

At about 7.30pm on 20 February 2004 a group of armed men raided the home of **Jabbar al-Badran** in Hay al-Andalus, Basra, and shot him dead. His son and daughter were also reportedly injured. Jabbar al-Badran had worked as a judge in the National Security Court until it was abolished by the Coalition Provisional Authority in May 2003. The court had been responsible for sentencing thousands of Iraqis to death and long terms of imprisonment after unfair trials often on the basis of confessions obtained by the use of torture.

Some Iraqis, including police officers, told Amnesty International that these killings were justified because Ba'athists and former government officials participated in the human rights violations of the former Iraqi government or provided information to security agencies which led to 'disappearances' and executions.

Amnesty International believes that it is fundamental for the countless victims of decades of grave violations of human rights by Iraqi government agents that those suspected of involvement are brought to justice as part of a process which conforms to international human rights law and standards. Executions in the street of people who may or may not have been responsible for past human rights violations does not bring Iraqis closer to securing truth, justice and accountability for past human rights violations. In fact, they make these goals even more difficult to achieve.

Killings of professionals

Many Iraqi professionals, including academics, medical doctors and lawyers, have been victims of assassination, but there has been no clear indication as to why they have been targeted or by whom. At least three senior professionals have been assassinated in Basra and many professionals in the city told Amnesty International delegates they feared for their lives.

Dr. Abdallah Hamed 'Abd al-Halim al-Fadhal, a surgeon aged 45, was appointed Deputy Dean for Scientific Affairs at the College of Medicine in Basra in 2001. He also worked as a consultant surgeon in Tahrir Hospital. On the afternoon of 20 September 2003 he was working in his private clinic in al-'Ashar. At about 7pm he left the clinic to have a word with another doctor. As he was speaking through a car window, a man approached him and said: 'Are you Dr. 'Abdallah?' He replied in the affirmative. The man then fired three rounds into the back of his head before escaping.

Dr. As'ad Salim 'Abd al-Qader, Dean of the Engineering Department, Basra University, and his colleague, Dr. Jasem Muhammad 'Abd al-Jabbar, were collected by a driver as usual from their homes on the morning of 4 October 2003. On their way to work, the car stopped at Dur al-Naft junction. Two men drew up on a motorcycle and opened fire, critically wounding Dr. As'ad Salim 'Abd al-Qader in the chest and injuring Dr. Jasem Muhammad 'Abd al-Jabbar.

In neither of these two cases was there any apparent motivation for the attacks.

Alcohol-related killings

Since the fall of the Iraqi government, people selling alcohol in Basra, whether legally or illegally, have been subjected to a campaign of intimidation, including violent attacks and targeted killings. According to Iraqi law, it is legal for licensed stores to sell alcohol. Before the start of the occupation, these licences were only issued to Christians. About 300 of the 1,150 Christian families living in Basra before the occupation used to earn their livelihoods from the alcohol trade, according to the Chaldean Archbishop of Basra and Southern Iraq, Monsignor Gibril Kassab.

Violence targeting those involved in the alcohol trade started soon after the occupation began. Shops selling music and videos have also been attacked. On 8 May 2003 two merchants, **'Abd al-Ahad Sleiwa and Sabah Kamel**, were shot dead in separate incidents. As a result of these killings, the licensed stores closed. Attacks, however, continued. **Sarkun Nanu Muradu** and **Bashir Toma Elias**, who both used to run liquor stores, were killed in November and December 2003 respectively. **Bashir Toma Elias**, 53, who shut down his liquor store in Bashar Street, Old Basra, after the two killings on 8 May, was shot dead on 24 December. A retired English teacher who drove a taxi to support his wife and six children, he had gone to the market in Old Basra at about 9am to do some shopping for the Christmas celebrations. According to his family, a man with a beard approached him and fired a bullet into the back of his neck.

The violence peaked on 15 February 2004, when at least nine people were killed by armed men who fired randomly into the crowded main street in Old Basra near the footbridge, a well-known spot for illegal selling of alcohol by street vendors. At least six others were seriously injured. Many of the wounded were neither selling nor buying alcohol. The dead included **Lo'ay Naser Hasab**, 43, unemployed; **Husam Samir Muhsen 'Abbas**, 19, a restaurant worker; **'Ali Kadhem 'Abbas**, a police officer; **Usama Shakr Rajab**, an upholsterer; **Naser Sabih Sa'id**; **Fayeq Naser Nati**; and **Sa'ad Muhammad 'Abd al-Khadhr**.

According to the Iraqi police, two other unidentified individuals were killed; their bodies were removed for burial before they could be transferred to the Office of Forensic Medicine.

One of those killed, Lo'ay Naser Hasab, had returned from exile in Iran to rejoin his wife and children. He had driven to Old Basra to shop for the family dinner. His son, Salwan Lo'ay Naser, and his brother-in-law, Ahmad Naser Shayyal, accompanied him. Lo'ay Naser Hasab parked near the footbridge where a small group of men were selling alcohol. He got out of the car and his son and brother-in-law waited. Two unmarked white pick-up trucks containing 12 to 13 men wearing balaclavas drove down the street, did a U-turn, and drove up the opposite side of the street. The men suddenly started to fire into the busy street. Some of them walked along the street shooting. According to Salwan Lo'ay Naser and Ahmad Naser Shayyal, the shooting continued for about 15 minutes. The men used a variety of arms, including a machine gun mounted on a pick-up truck, rifles and pistols. Lo'ay Naser Hasab was hit in his temple, shoulder and lower back, and died shortly afterwards in Basra General Hospital.

Husam Samir Muhsen 'Abbas also died in the attack. A young man who worked in a local restaurant, he was responsible for supporting his disabled father and seven brothers and sisters. His maternal cousin, Murtada Salman Za'lan, 23, who was with him in the area, told Amnesty International: '[A]t some point between 6pm and 6.15pm, I heard the sound of gunfire. It lasted for about three minutes. I ran back to the source of the fire. I found Husam lying on the ground. He had been hit in the left side and the round had gone through his right side and through his right arm. I saw about 20 other people, including women and children, lying wounded on the ground on both sides of the road. I took Husam myself to Basra General Hospital. He was then transferred to Basra Teaching Hospital. Husam was bleeding internally. He underwent an operation but the doctors could not stop the internal bleeding and he died about two hours later.' Murtada Salman Za'lan added: 'We just want to know who did this but there is no result... We want the story of what happened to be published in the Iraqi newspapers. Until now no Iraqi newspaper or the local radio has talked about what happened.'

According to Archbishop Gibril Kassab, about 150 Christian families, many of whom were involved in the alcohol trade, have relocated to their original homes in and around Mosul in northern Iraq. He estimated that 20 or 30 families had left Basra permanently and the others plan to return if the security situation in Basra stabilizes.

Many people interviewed by Amnesty International blamed Islamist groups for the attacks, although no group has claimed responsibility. A senior Iraqi police official confirmed in February 2004 to Amnesty International that no prosecutions had been initiated for killings of alcohol vendors.

Investigations

There appears to have been virtually no investigations or prosecutions of political killings by individuals and armed groups since the occupation began. The Iraqi

Police Service, which effectively collapsed in April 2003, remains ineffective, especially when dealing with complex crimes such as political killings. Many Iraqis interviewed by Amnesty International lacked confidence in the police's ability to provide security in southern Iraq. With regard to political killings, police officers interviewed by Amnesty International generally expressed the view that these cases were unsolvable because they had been committed by unidentified individuals and because eyewitnesses would not come forward. Generally, it appears that no initiatives by the Iraqi police to prevent such killings have been taken. Amnesty International did learn that the British Army and Iraqi police have undertaken joint patrols at night in recent months in the Casino Lebanon area to prevent dumping of corpses and that this measure had been successful. Amnesty International was unable to identify a single case in Basra city where a perpetrator of a political killing had been brought to trial.

Some police officers clearly did not regard conducting investigations into the killings of people linked to the Ba'ath Party as a priority or even a responsibility for the police. The head of one police station told an Amnesty International delegate that people 'were in the right' for seeking to avenge the deaths of their relatives who had 'disappeared' or been executed by the previous Iraqi government. Other police officers recognized, however, the threat that this phenomenon placed to the rule of law and human rights.

The capacity of the Iraqi Police Service in southern Iraq has been strengthened since May 2003. Offices have been renovated and re-equipped but the police still do not have sufficient mobile communications equipment or vehicles. There are now more police officers in both Basra and Maysan provinces, although some had no police training before they were recruited and lack policing skills. Both these and experienced police officers need to be trained if they are to meet new demands for policing based on respect for human rights and democratic values.

The challenges facing the Iraqi Police Service are greater than ever before. Police are expected to be accountable and operate in accordance with Iraqi law and international human rights standards. They are expected to tackle serious crime, including violent crime, which has dramatically increased since the fall of the Iraqi government. In the past the police frequently secured criminal convictions on the basis of confessions, often obtained through the use of torture and ill-treatment. Now the Iraqi police must rely increasingly on other sorts of evidence, such as eyewitness testimony and forensic evidence. However, as was frankly acknowledged by the Coalition Provisional Authority's Head of Law and Order, there is 'a huge gap in investigation procedures, which is a highly skilled and specialized art requiring specialized training'.

Police in southern Iraq also face threats and physical intimidation, even killing, for carrying out their duties. They are aware that in other parts of Iraq, hundreds of Iraqi police have been killed by armed groups.

On 20 February 2004, the Coalition Provisional Authority's Head of Law and Order for southern Iraq told Amnesty International delegates that strengthening the capacity of the Iraqi Police Service, as well as other Iraqi security forces, was the top priority of the British Army in southern Iraq. An array of training programmes has been set up for newly recruited police, as well as veterans. The British Army and the Coalition Provisional Authority aim to support the police during their operations and through the provision of training and equipment. As part of this process the British Army, including the Royal Military Police, has embedded personnel in the police to mentor them.

International standards

International human rights law obligates states to protect individuals against human rights abuses, including abuses of the right to life, committed by individuals or organizations. For example, Article 2(1) of the International Covenant on Civil and Political Rights requires the United Kingdom to ensure to everyone the rights guaranteed in the Covenant. States must exercise due diligence in preventing, investigating, prosecuting and providing an effective remedy for abuses of the right to life. If they fail to do so, they will be regarded under international law as being responsible for these abuses and in breach of their international obligations. Article 27 of the Fourth Geneva Convention also requires the United Kingdom, as an occupying power, to protect Iraqis, particularly from threats and acts of violence.

Armed groups are themselves required to respect minimum standards of international humanitarian law, justice and humanity, including a prohibition on deliberate or indiscriminate attacks on civilians.

Conclusions and recommendations

On 7 January 2004 the United Kingdom Minister of State for the Armed Forces stated that UK forces 'are working in partnership with the Iraqi people to establish a safe and secure environment, and are doing so under the rule of law.' This is not the picture found by Amnesty International delegates in Iraq. As this report has shown, in certain cases UK armed forces have opened fire and killed Iraqi civilians in breach of international human rights standards relating to the use of force and firearms. Moreover, the British Army's response to suspected unlawful killing of civilians has undermined, rather than upheld, the rule of law. It has failed to conduct investigations into all killings of civilians, and the investigations that have been carried out have failed to ensure that 'justice was done and seen to be done' in the eyes of victims' families or the Iraqi or UK public. The investigations have been shrouded in secrecy – some victims have not even been aware that they have been opened. Families of victims have also not been given adequate information on how to apply for compensation.

Amnesty International also believes that the UK armed forces and the Iraqi Police Service have failed many of the families of people who have been killed by individuals and armed groups. They have failed by not exercising due diligence in preventing such abuses or in investigating, prosecuting and punishing those who carried out the killings.

Amnesty International welcomes the efforts of United Kingdom and other governments to strengthen the capacity of the Iraqi Police Service. However, increased capacity must be matched by an increased willingness by the police to take action in such cases and uphold the rule of law.

Amnesty International calls on the UK authorities, the Coalition Provisional Authority and the Iraqi Governing Council to:
- Ensure that all individuals exercising law enforcement functions, whether members of the UK forces or the Iraqi police, secure the right to life through respect for the Code of Conduct for Law Enforcement Officials, the UN Basic Principles on the Use of Force and Firearms, and principles of humanitarian law. Law enforcement officials should employ lethal force only when strictly unavoidable in order to protect life.
- Provide training to law enforcement officials, including military forces acting in that capacity, in the use of graduated force and firearms.
- Equip law enforcement officials, including military forces acting in that capacity, with self-defensive equipment in order to reduce the need to use firearms.
- Ensure that investigations are conducted into all suspected cases of unlawful killings of civilians by law enforcement officials, including military forces acting in that capacity.
- Ensure that such investigations are thorough, competent, impartial and independent, and seen to be so.
- Ensure that such investigations include an adequate autopsy, as well as collection and analysis of all physical and documentary evidence and statements from witnesses.
- Ensure that the results of such investigations are made public.
- Bring to justice in fair trials anyone reasonably suspected of responsibility for unlawful killings.
- Provide reparation, including payment of adequate compensation, to the families of people unlawfully killed by law enforcement officials, including military forces acting in that capacity.
- Keep families of victims of unlawful killings informed of the procedure for applying for compensation and of the progress of investigations into the killing.
- Exercise due diligence in preventing unlawful killings, as well as investigating, bringing to justice and punishing all individuals who carry out such abuses.
- Deliver civic education about community safety to counter cultures of violence.

Amnesty International calls on the UK authorities to:
- Make public the Rules of Engagement for Operation Telic.
- Ensure that UK forces can communicate effectively with Iraqi civilians by ensuring that competent interpreters are available.

- Establish a civilian-led mechanism to investigate all suspected killings by UK forces. Such a mechanism should be capable of applying international human rights law and standards relevant to the investigations of allegations of serious human rights violations by the military.
- Consider appointing liaison officers to act as a focal point of contact between families of people killed by UK forces on the one hand and the British Army and Coalition Provisional Authority on the other.

Amnesty International calls on all armed groups operating in Iraq to:
- Respect minimum standards of international humanitarian law, justice and humanity, including the prohibition on deliberate attacks on civilians, indiscriminate attacks and hostage-taking.

Amnesty International calls on the international community to:
- Prioritize the mobilization of international efforts to rebuild the capacity of the international civilian police force, as required by UN Security Council Resolution 1483.

Notes

1 On 4 April US forces launched major operations in Falluja following the killing, burning and mutilation of four US private security guards by insurgents on 31 March.
2 Oxford Research International Ltd., 'National Survey of Iraq, February 2004', p. 6.
3 Amnesty International, 'Iraq: Amnesty International condemns latest bombings,' (News Service No. 51. (MDE 14/003/20040).
4 Section 2(2) CPA Order 17.
5 These claims presumably include claims related to deaths in custody and deaths caused by traffic accidents, as well as deaths arising from shooting incidents.
6 The UK is a party to the Fourth Geneva Convention and Protocol I.
7 The Human Rights Committee, set up under the ICCPR, and other bodies monitoring the implementation by states of their human rights obligations under the treaties they have ratified, have consistently ruled that such obligations extend to any territory in which a state exercises jurisdiction or control, including territories occupied as a result of military action.
8 The European Court of Human Rights has recognized the extra-territorial applicability of the ECHR in situations where a state party exercises all or some public powers normally to be exercised by the government of a territory through the state party's effective control of the relative territory and its inhabitants as a consequence of *inter alia* military occupation. See Bankovic v. the United Kingdom, para. 71.
9 See Margaret McCann v. the United Kingdom, para. 161, and Hugh Jordan v. the United Kingdom, para 105.
10 The name of the victim has been changed to protect his relatives.

Copyright ©Amnesty International

MORE MISSING PAGES – THE TAGUBA REPORT

On 24 May 2004, Associated Press filed the following report under the headline 'Senate Copy of Report On Abuse May Be Short'.

2,000 Pages Missing, Committee Aides Say

At least 2,000 pages might have been missing from the copy of the Army report on soldiers' abusive treatment of Iraqi prisoners that was delivered to the Senate Armed Services Committee.

The 6,000-page report, compiled by Maj. Gen. Antonio M. Taguba, formed the basis for hearings this month into the allegations. Taguba found 'numerous incidents of sadistic, blatant and wanton criminal abuses' had been inflicted on Iraqis held at Abu Ghraib prison outside Baghdad between last October and December.

Pentagon spokesman Lawrence Di Rita said he knew of no contact with the Pentagon by anybody at the committee about the reported missing pages. He said he understood there may have been a computer glitch that made some of the electronically stored pages difficult to open, but the problem was resolved. 'Certainly, if there is some shortfall in what was provided, it was an oversight,' Di Rita said in a statement.

Time magazine reported yesterday that committee aides noticed the report was missing a third of its pages after they divided the document and its 106 annexes into separate binders, stacking them and comparing the stack with an already counted stack of 6,000 pages.

One committee member, Sen. Pat Roberts (R-Kan.), said yesterday he would talk to the chairman, Sen. John W. Warner (R-Va.), to get the facts. 'I don't know' whether pages are missing, Roberts said, 'but we'll sure ... find out.' Roberts heads the Senate intelligence committee, which also has been given the report.

Sen. Jack Reed (D-R.I.), another Armed Services Committee member, said he became aware Friday of the possibility of the missing pages. Reed, who appeared with Roberts on CBS's 'Face the Nation' yesterday, indicated he would not be surprised if it were true because of the way, he said, that the Defense Department usually treats Congress. 'There's a lack of cooperation. There's a lack of candor. And that has hurt not only their perception but also gives rise to feelings or inferences that something is amiss deliberately,' Reed said. 'I hope that's not the case.'

'Last November in Iraq, I travelled to Fallujah during the early days of what would become known as the "Ramadan Offensive" ... I enquired of a young man there why the people of that city were attacking Americans more frequently each day. How many of the attacks, I wanted to know, were carried out by foreign fighters? How many by local Islamists? ...

The young man – I'll call him Salih – listened, answered patiently in his limited but eloquent English, but soon became impatient with what he plainly saw as my American obsession with categories and particulars. Finally he interrupted my litany of questions, pushed his face close to mine, and spoke to me slowly and emphatically:

For Fallujans it is a *shame* to have foreigners break down their doors. It is a *shame* for them to have foreigners stop and search their women. It is a *shame* for the foreigners to put a bag over their heads, to make a man lie on the ground with your shoe on his neck. This is a great *shame*, you understand? This is a great *shame* for the whole tribe.

It is the *duty* of that man, and of that tribe, to get revenge on this soldier – to kill that man. Their duty is to attack them, to *wash the shame*. The shame is a *stain*, a dirty thing; they have to *wash* it. No sleep – we cannot sleep until we have revenge. They have to kill soldiers.

He leaned back and looked at me, then tried one more time. "The Americans," he said, "*provoke* the people. They don't *respect* the people."'

Torture and Truth, Mark Danner, *The New York Review of Books*, June 2004

PCS campaigns for:

Public and
Commercial
Services Union

work-life balance
fair pay and pensions
improved public services

We oppose racism, fascism and all forms of inequality

We stand for peace, social justice, international solidarity
and freedom for all oppressed peoples

Janice Godrich
President

Mark Serwotka
General Secretary

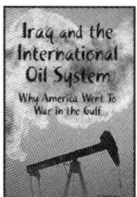

Iraq and the International Oil System:
Why America Went to War in the Gulf

Stephen C. Pelletière

How the Gulf came under the control of a coercive cartel - The history of the oil system that evolved in the United States - The role of oil in conflicts in Central Asia- Motivations behind the most recent war in Iraq.; 254pp.
Pbk   ISBN 0 85036 551 1   £14.95

THE MAKING OF A CYBERTARIAT:
Virtual Work in a Real World
Foreword by Colin Leys   Ursula Huws

A new global labour force is being created working in call centres, homes and electronic sweatshops. New technologies are also transforming daily life. This book presents a coherent conceptual framework within which these developments can be understood. 208pp Pbk   ISBN 0 85036 537 6   £ 13.95

AVAILABLE POST FREE in the UK FROM: MERLIN PRESS
P O Box 30705, London, WC2E 8QD

Routledge Classics

Get inside one of the greatest minds of the 20th Century

Six Bertrand Russell titles publishing February 2004

'There is no one who uses the English language more beguilingly than Russell, no one smoothes the kinks and creases more artfully out of the most crumpled weaves of thought.' - *The Times*

Prices from £7.99 to £12.99

Available from all good bookshops or visit www.routledgeclassics.com

Also published in Routledge Classics...

Adorno ... Andersen ... Barth ... Blake ... Bohm ... Buber ... Derrida ... Durkheim ... Eagleton ... Einstein ... Foucault ... Freud ... Fromm ... Grimm ... Hayek ... Jameson ... Jung ... Kermode ... Lacan ... Lear ... Lévi-Strauss ... Lorenz ... McLuhan ... Marcuse ... Mauss ... Merleau-Ponty ... Midgley ... Murdoch ... Piaget ... Popper ... Ricoeur ... Sartre ... Weber ... Weil ... Wittgenstein ...Yeats

More than 100 titles available

Reviews

Empire

Michael Hardt & Antonio Negri, *Empire*, Harvard University Press, 2000, 478 pages, hardback ISBN 0674251210, £25.95, paperback ISBN 0674006712, £12.95
David Harvey, *The New Imperialism*, Oxford University Press, 2003, 253 pages, hardback ISBN 0199264317, £16.99

Empire, and the American empire in particular, has become a favourite subject of study by historians, economists, sociologists and even philosophers and literary critics. Indeed, so many writers about the American empire have begun to refer back to a book published in the year 2000 by the Italian philosopher Antonio Negri, together with the American professor of Literature, Michael Hardt, simply titled 'Empire', that it seems to have become required reading for students of imperialism. Opening the book of 478 pages, it appears that by the year 2002 a twelfth printing had been necessary. So this review may seem somewhat out of date to some *Spokesman* readers. It should be of considerable interest, however, to supporters of the World Social Forum and seems to have inspired the *Guardian* columnist, George Monbiot, in his latest book, *Manifesto for a New World Order*. This is because of Hardt's and Negri's faith in the 'multitude' which 'will magically rise up to inherit the earth', as David Harvey summarises their conclusions. At the other pole, *Empire* has been welcomed by the US State Department's semi-official publication *Foreign Affairs*. This in turn is because Hardt and Negri see American empire as fulfilling Thomas Jefferson's judgement of the US Constitution: 'I am persuaded no constitution was ever before so well calibrated as ours for extensive empire and self-government.'

Hardt and Negri start from the claim that the US empire is unlike previous imperialisms because it has no territorial fixes. With 725 US military bases dotted about the earth's surface, not to mention all the US satellites circling the earth, that would seem to be debatable. The point they are making is rather that the US empire is not limited in territory, as previous empires were, but is universal. More than this, empire is what they call 'bio-political', generating 'bio-power', that is to say, not only political and economic, but social and cultural influence embracing the whole person of all those living on the planet. Coercion is needed, but that is only to ensure that all can enjoy Jefferson's promise of self-government. This allows for the 'moral intervention' not only of religious and other non-governmental organisations, but of inter-national government agencies and the US government itself. Hardt and Negri write of this empire as it 'extends and consolidates the model of network power' – the networks of capital, labour and technology.

Hardt and Negri see the nation states withering away as prime movers and remaining only as agents of international capital, but there is a pyramid of national power with the United States at the pinnacle, holding hegemony over the global use of force. This is not to say, they insist, that the US provides a transcendent centre of capital. It presides over a network. In language that is deeply opaque, they write:

> 'Through the social development of capital, the mechanisms of modern sovereignty – the processes of coding, overcoding and recoding that imposed a transcendent order over a bounded and segmented social terrain – are progressively replaced by an *axiomatic,* that is, a set of equations and relationships that determines and combines variables and coefficients immediately and equally across terrains without reference to prior and fixed definitions of terms' (*Empire*, pp.326-7).

Make what you can of that! They are presumably referring to the working of world markets. But David Harvey reminds us that markets are heavily influenced by monetary regimes, which are very much in the 'transcendent' hands of the Wall Street-US Treasury-IMF complex.

The whole thrust of the argument in the Hardt and Negri book is that since the days of the Caesars and absolute monarchs we have looked at empires ruled from the top downwards. The rule of capital, however, has to be seen from below, responding always, whether by control or consent, to the initiatives of labour, positive or negative. This argument is all the more telling today, when capital movements have become not only increasingly global, but increasingly free of nation state controls. At the same time they aver that 'In empire and its regime of bio-power, economic production and political constitution tend increasingly to coincide' (*Empire*, page 41). In what they call the 'post-modern age' the base and superstructure of Marx's model become merged. The main reason for this is not so much the change in capital, though that is ever more global in operation, but the change in labour.

The change in the nature of the proletariat, that is to say all those exploited by capital, results from what Hardt and Negri see as the development of network production in which communication lies at the centre of production, communication that has no need for Marx's mass workers and no territorial limits. The bargaining power of individual workers, skilled or mass, disappears, but at the same time what was for Marx 'variable capital', labour becomes an 'autonomous agent of production', logging onto the network at will. One has to stop at this point and ask whether, since in production capital owns the network of pay, there is not some conflict of ideas here. Hardt and Negri understand perfectly that 'Capitalism sets in motion a continuous cycle of private reappropriation of public goods: the expropriation of what was common.' (*Empire*, page 301). So, where lies the proletariat's autonomy?

We have to turn to David Harvey, whose work Hardt and Negri quote to explain the new hierarchies in capitalist accumulation and commodification (*Empire*, page 154). After the abstruse and convoluted language of Hardt and Negri, the clear and simple English of David Harvey is a joy to read. He starts by asking what drove the Bush government into the war in Iraq. Was it to reinforce the position of a non-elected President, was it to divert attention from growing social problems at home, was it to control the dwindling reserves of oil, was it to boost a failing economy? Harvey believes that all these factors played a part but that there are deeper political/economic developments to be understood. These arise from the contradictions inherent in the capitalist system, most particularly the over-accumulation of capital, not just from the falling consumption of exploited workers, but more seriously from the failing opportunities for profitable investment. Following Rosa Luxemburg, Harvey believes that capital needs always to expand, requiring fields somewhere 'outside' the system, at first in undeveloped regions and then where?

David Harvey's book contains a long section on 'How America's Power Grew'. This is a story of continuous territorial expansion into the whole North American continent, followed by extension of power first in the rest of the Americas and then world-wide. But Harvey follows Giovanni Arrighi in distinguishing the capitalist logic of power which has no bounds and the territorial logic which requires a spatial fix. These two logics do not always coincide, and may conflict. A good example is the failure of Joseph Chamberlain at the beginning of the Twentieth Century to convert the City of London to the idea of imperial preference. British capital was interested in investment opportunities in the whole world, not just in the British Empire. Capitalist competition always tends towards monopoly positions in any region, but a monopoly of the whole world market implies the danger of overreach, such as brought down all earlier empires – Rome, Venice, Holland, Britain. With over 700 bases, with military expenditure exceeding that of many other states combined and with escalating costs of the occupation of Iraq, the United States too may be approaching its nemesis.

It is David Harvey's revision of Marx's theory of capitalist crisis that is most interesting. Marx assumed that capital accumulation proceeded through expanded reproduction, so long as the necessary conditions were in place – of private property, free markets, guarantees of contract, law and order, a trustworthy money as both store of value and means of exchange, and a facilitating state. Primitive accumulation – by theft and tribute and the expropriation of the commons – was relegated to an earlier stage of capitalist development. Harvey, by contrast, sees such predatory practices as persistent and continuous and gives examples: the privatisation of public assets, mergers and acquisitions of companies, asset stripping and asset destruction through inflation, raiding of pension funds, corporate fraud, and credit and stock manipulations. These he summarise as 'accumulation by dispossession', the problem for capital being that the process requires increasing coercion in place of the consent on which capitalists have always relied for their legitimation.

It is this shift in United States foreign policy from hegemony by consent to domination by coercion that Harvey believes marks the change under the Bush regime from the influence of neo-libs to neo-cons. He seems to be remarkably optimistic that if liberal Europe will just give the liberal forces in America the benefit of the doubt, then these forces will be successful in their struggle to curb the current militarism in US government circles. Perhaps Hardt and Negri have in mind the same hope when they write in what I can only call 'gobbledegook':

> 'On the terrain of production and regulation of subjectivity, and in the disjunction between the political subject and the economic subject, it seems that we can identify a real field of struggle in which all the gambits of the constitution and the equilibria among forces can be reopened – a true and proper situation of crisis and maybe eventually of revolution.' (*Empire* page 321)

Harvey's fears, which he expresses writing in his last pages, are that the spread of world-wide anti-American feelings will, he thinks, only make the struggle against militarism all the harder. The revelations in recent weeks of the use of torture by US forces in Iraq must surely reinforce his fears. But it is at least possible that such anti-American revulsion may on the contrary serve to turn Americans away from the whole Empire project.

Michael Barratt Brown

Whitewash on fast spin

Simon Rogers (editor), *The Hutton Inquiry and its Impact*, Guardian Books with Politico's Publishing, 2004, 400 pages, paperback ISBN 1842751069, £7.99

It's nice for a change, but a bit harder, doing a review of a book that's already getting a good showing in the bookshops, and on an issue that keeps developing. The issues are so important that the book deserves the widest possible circulation, and close reading. It's well organised and edited too, for a quick publication, though I'd have preferred even more nuggets of information, and an index, and maybe a bit less of *The Guardian* think pieces, since we already get the gist of them in the daily paper.

On the issues, it's obvious that the general reception to Hutton has been that it was a whitewash job, even though speculation during the inquiry process hyped it up as potentially terminal for Blair and Campbell and Hoon and some of the top dogs in the cloak and dagger world of intelligence. I didn't think this was at all likely: in the British system, judges do not bring down governments, even if maybe they ought to have a due role in triggering such a process.

So whitewash was expected, but for me something bigger happened, too. I think Hutton was weak-wristed with the whitewash but, more importantly, was the servant of some very strategic spin..

Before explaining what I mean by strategic spin, can I also say that the whitewash – to experienced observers – was maybe deliberately pretty thin. Was it designed, perhaps, to offer only a minimum veil of protection to Blair,

Campbell and Hoon? Was there an element of 'Blair futures' about it all? My sense is that if there was a halfway credible successor to Brown as Chancellor, which is all that big business really bothers about, then Blair would be well on his way by now. Not that a change at the top would make much difference to policy, of course.

But back to big spin: this has two aims. Firstly, there is damage limitation, which is essential for people in public life who make cock-ups. And secondly, so called 'closure', or 'moving on' to another agenda. (Incidentally, 'closure', which sounds very posh and formal, has its origins in pulp romance fiction and soap television series where one romance partner needs to be finished off – 'closed' – in order to introduce another lover and keep the reader's attention from probing too deeply ...)

The hard bit of this review is that things have truly moved on since Hutton, so we can't read the book the same way that we might have read it a few days after the Report came out. Now we have two big events to take into consideration. Both are central to the developing story, and both involve strategic spin.

One was Clare Short's revelation about the United Kingdom (and the United States) spying on Kofi Annan's office. The other was the Madrid bombings and the political response of the Spanish electorate. Both fit my theme of spin being more important than whitewash. Or, to be more formal, that decoding spin matters more to effective political opposition than complaining about whitewash.

The spin in the United Nations spying revelation was to try and see that no one asked what the spying was for. It was presented as somehow routine if regrettable. I owe to Ken Coates of the Russell Foundation the instant perception that the spying was to find out about, and disrupt, the peace plan being designed by the small countries at the United Nations to head off the United States/United Kingdom invasion plans.

The Aznar Government's handling of the Madrid bombings shows spin coming wonderfully unstuck, when the people, aided by the practical experience of the rescue workers on the scene, saw that the blame-game against ETA was a cover up to avoid electoral punishment for Aznar going to war alongside Bush and Blair. My guess is that the international focus group consultants had told Aznar that he would suffer electoral punishment, and the ETA blame tactic was not spontaneous.

So, what of the spins around the Hutton Report and the death of Dr Kelly?

First comes the idea that we are governed by well-meaning folk, who keep honest and candid diaries, but can't always manage formal minutes of meetings; who, even in matters as important as going to war and undermining international law as we understood it, are so busy with other routine matters of government that they only have one or two key, and, in the circumstances, rather casual, open-attendance meetings to deal with a massive political crisis.

The spun idea of well-meanings and honest folk at the top was structurally sustained by the choice – in the sense of 'choice' or 'select' fruit and vegetables – of e-mails presented to Hutton. These carefully protected the back, for example, of Jonathan Powell, Blair's Chief of Staff and, incidentally, the younger brother of Mrs Thatcher's foreign policy guru. It rested on the modest volume of written evidence, which, if I am right, was invited, not demanded, and treated at face value. I stress the point: it was highly selective. Or, to put the point more bluntly, its status as evidence was as little to be trusted as would be the volunteered evidence of a hardened criminal that he or she 'wasn't there, your honour, and I've got a bit of paper to prove it, and you'll have to take my word for it'.

But the alternative, of commanded and examined and investigated paperwork and telephone tapes, would have been a nightmare for them all. We have only to remember what happened to Nixon in the Watergate Inquiry.

And on the status of telephone evidence, incidentally, it is important to the Hutton judgment (page 314 of the book) that Dr Kelly told a friend that his leak was unauthorised in a telephone conversation. Questions about other people's phone conversations should have been in order. And tapes too.

Finally, on paperwork, the top policeman giving evidence reported that Dr Kelly's computers would have printed out a pile of paper twice as high as Big Ben. While this was no doubt meant to explain why this couldn't be evidence, we are asked to believe in the authority and representativeness of the modest quantity of self-selected paperwork from the top folk, who number dozens in comparison to a single technical expert.

So, I don't think the personal paperwork proved anything of consequence, but I can't name names because it might let somebody sue. Which calls to mind the case of Mr Campbell, in which I take the common view that it remains interesting that he didn't seem too keen to sue Mr Gilligan. That might have meant the diaries were examined under different rules. Or maybe it would have undermined the longer term value of the memoirs.

The spin of a nothing-to-hide and truly open government was further sustained by the appearance from the shadows of top intelligence officials in their best suits showing that our spies are really nice guys who are much deserving of their salaries from the taxpayers.

So, spin number one was to make us believe that we are governed by straightforward folk with nothing to hide in a workaday sort of political toy-town. Toy-town or nasty-town? Page 217 of the book records Dr Kelly's e-mail about 'many dark actors playing games' only hours before his death..

Spin number two, for me, concerns the matter of Dr Kelly being the sole, single source of the leak about the weapons of mass destruction evidence. The whole thing was narrowed down to the Gilligan report and Dr Kelly. My instinct is that right across the huge government machine people were leaking like mad, unauthorised, semi-authorised, accurate and misleading, and including auto-authorised leaks by people who wanted to protect their backs from potential disaster, and a war that remains deeply unpopular with some of the military and the top folk, quite apart from the public at large. Readers may like to follow the paper trail on this theme: strangely enough, the question of 'source' is at the heart of the WMD dossier issue itself, as well as being central to the question of who leaked. I seem to recall that Dr Kelly thought he might be 'a' source, but note that he rapidly became 'the' source. No wonder he felt threatened.

The third spin can be put simply, but it is very important. It is that this was an entirely British affair, driven, if not well, by Mr Blair and those whose proper job it is to run the country and conduct wars and all that. I make the point bluntly: since Blair was the Siamese twin of Bush, you'd have thought some speculation might have taken place about what the Americans did, and did not do, and think about it all.

It would have been too much to hope for the truth from an inquiry. And aspirations about future inquiries must be at rock bottom. If we feel powerless, and come to expect whitewash, maybe we can take some heart, too. Recent times have shown that spin doesn't always limit damage, or achieve closure. So trying to de-code it can have some effect in checking the power of politicians. It may be a bit complicated, but it can work as long as we also just keep on asking the simple questions. For example, why did Campbell go when he apparently did no wrong? How can a secretary of state for defence not know or recollect the meaning of something as crucial as which weapons had the 45 minute tag? And, less easily, what would have happened if Dr Kelly had lived? Would the leaks have stopped? Would there have been closure?

Regan Scott

Bush and Blair

Bob Woodward, *Plan of Attack*, Simon and Schuster, 467 pages, hardback ISBN 074325547X , £18.99

Bob Woodward gives us the nearest thing we have had up to now of a fly on the wall account of how President Bush and Tony Blair came to launch their invasion of Iraq.

Woodward interviewed seventy-five of the key conspirators, and talked for three and a half hours with President Bush. He reveals what he could discover about the war plans, as they evolved, and portrays the principal actors with incisive economy.

The day before Thanksgiving, on November 21st 2001, Bush met with Rumsfeld for a discussion 'in the utmost privacy'. 'What kind of war plan do you have for Iraq? How do you feel about the war plan for Iraq?' Rumsfeld did not think much of the existing plan: it did not represent the ideas of General Tommy Franks, and it 'certainly didn't represent his own thinking'.

It was, says Woodward, 'Desert Storm II +'. The trouble was that it takes years to draft war plans. 'The process was woefully broken and maddeningly slow. He was working to fix it.' '"Let's get started on this" Bush recalled saying. "And get

Tommy Franks looking at what it would take to protect America by removing Saddam Hussein if we have to."'

The President was keen to know whether all of this could be done without attracting too much attention. But when Rumsfeld went to work, all the massive resources of the American military, Full Spectrum Dominance and all, were bent to this one pressing task.

By the following August, General Franks and his colleagues were ready to report on the reworked plans. This was no ideological blueprint: within the military mindset, it was necessary to destroy 4,000 possible targets, which would need 12,000 to 13,000 separate weapons. 'A large building or complex might have four to twelve individual "aim points" for individual weapons – bombs or missiles'. In the Franks plan there were one hundred and thirty-odd targets with high collateral damage, 'which was defined as possibly killing thirty or more civilians'. Rumsfeld would have liked to minimise that danger, and he told Franks to review the estimate and reassess it.

All this, involving the appropriate legions of military planners, was firmly unwinding before Tony Blair arrived in Washington to insist on the validation of the whole schema with a United Nations Resolution.

This is the story of the hatching of a war crime and it offers significant evidence for a future tribunal of investigation. In particular, it shows the lengths to which Bush was prepared to go in order to provide propitious circumstances for Blair to bring his forces on side in the coming invasion. It also documents in some detail the negotiations with Prince Bandar, the Saudi Ambassador. Blair was desperate that Bush should not say anything to frighten the children in the House of Commons, before he had got his vote for war. Bandar's anxieties, by contrast, were that Bush might be prevailed upon to postpone his war if the Iraqis were to offer concessions acceptable within the majority of Security Council Members.

They got their war. They 'won' it quickly. But domination did not follow, and is highly likely not to follow. Instead, it is likely that both Bush and his satellites will fall, while new and unforeseen uncertainties blanket the Middle East and trouble the world.

R. Thomas

Will civilisation survive?

Robert Hinde and Joseph Rotblat, ***War No More: Eliminating Conflict in the Nuclear Age*,** **Pluto Press, 2003, paper ISBN 0745321917, £10.95**

I can remember sitting in meetings in the 1980s when debate raged as to whether CND was a 'pacifist' organisation. 'Definitely not', said many who spoke for the movement, 'we are nuclear pacifists'. Now we have this book, which clearly states that in the nuclear age we cannot risk war. It is not just enough to ban weapons of mass destruction, and especially nuclear weapons, but war itself must be eliminated.

It is interesting to see, also, how the views of others have moved on. The Foreword to *War No More* is written by Robert McNamara. This is the man who was part of the team which agreed a strategy of fire-bombing 67 Japanese cities, killing upwards of 1.9 million civilians. He later played key roles in the Cuba crisis and the Vietnam war. Yet he commends the book, and endorses the authors' aim of looking at 'how war can be abolished or, at a minimum, how the risk of war can be reduced'.

All those involved would want the widest possible audience for *War No More*. The very opening sentence states that 'This book is written to convince you, the reader, that if our civilization – indeed, the human species – is to survive in this nuclear age, war of all types will have to be abolished and peaceful means found to solve disputes.'

The authors tackle the oft-repeated justification for the retention of nuclear weapons: '...the generally held belief that a third world war was prevented by the existence of nuclear warheads, and that their presence in the arsenals is no cause for worry, is an illusion.' Contrast that, and the expanded arguments in the Nuclear Peril chapter, with statements from, for example, NATO's Strategic Concept (published in 1999 and unchanged): 'nuclear weapons preserve the peace' and 'NATO will maintain, at the minimum level consistent with the prevailing security environment, adequate (nuclear) sub-strategic forces in Europe'. Indeed, the Trident nuclear-armed submarines are 'integrated' into NATO and the US NATO forces keep nuclear warheads on at least seven bases in NATO states, including in the United Kingdom, at Lakenheath in Suffolk, and in Turkey. According to the authors, the fact that there has not yet been a nuclear exchange in a conflict must be put down 'more to good luck than good management'.

What is to be done? The authors are keen to promote peace education, arms control treaties, conflict resolution, and confidence building. They look at the role of intervention and the United Nations and the whole question of world governance. They certainly see that campaigning has a role, in which groups such as the CND, (Campaign for Nuclear Disarmament) and CAAT (Campaign Against the Arms Trade) must surely have key roles. In support of Hinde's and Rotblat's arguments, the group Movement for the Abolition of War has produced an educational video entitled 'War No More', with an accompanying booklet and guidelines for discussion.*

Rae Street

---

*Available from Movement for the Abolition of War, 11 Venetia Road, London N4 1EJ www.abolishwar.org.uk price £8.

Amicus fighting for the liberty of working people at home and abroad

Joint General Secretary
Derek Simpson

Joint General Secretary
Roger Lyons